The Jewish Centaur

The Jewish Centaur

ADVENTURES IN PENTECOSTAL SPIRITUALITY

_____

Joshua Rice

CASCADE *Books* · Eugene, Oregon

THE JEWISH CENTAUR
Adventures in Pentecostal Spirituality

Cascade Books
An Imprint of Wipf and Stock Publishers
199 W. 8th Ave., Suite 3
Eugene, OR 97401

www.wipfandstock.com

ISBN 13: 978-1-62564-624-8

Cataloguing-in-Publication Data

Rice, Joshua

The Jewish centaur : adventures in pentecostal spirituality / Joshua Rice.

x + 122 p. ; 23 cm. Includes bibliographical references.

ISBN 13: 978-1-62564-624-8

1. Rice, Joshua. 2. Spiritual biography. I. Title.

PS3604.O434 R53 2015

Manufactured in the U.S.A.   10/28/2015

For my mother

Contents

Acknowledgments

There are several individuals and institutions who deserve personal gratitude for playing a role in the contents of this memoir. To the faculty of Lee University and Pentecostal Theological Seminary, especially Rickie Moore, Chris Thomas, Cheryl Johns, Sang Ehil Han, and Lee Roy Martin, thank you for introducing me to a Pentecostal theology worth falling in love with. Knowing all of you is like being a seminarian all over again—a feeling I have attempted to recapture in these pages. Likewise, to my friends at Columbia Theological Seminary and the Lutheran School of Theology at Chicago, I hope you will take this book's banter as good fun. It is only because you gave me the space to explore my own story in the context of yours that these discoveries were possible.

On the ecclesiastical side, I would like to thank the wonderful members of my present parish—Mount Paran North Church of God in Marietta, Georgia. In the middle of the Bible belt of Baptist country, you remind me that Pentecostal practice and witness remain both relevant and meaningful to regular folks like us with bills and kids. I would especially like to express appreciation to Madeline Mulkey, hailing from our congregation but now a student at Wheaton College, for her lucid feedback and editorial work on the initial manuscript. I have no doubt she has a literary career waiting just round the bend.

I retain the most sacred honors for the members of my family who began forging our Pentecostal heritage long before such a lifestyle was at all fashionable. To my parents and my wife's parents, thank you for raising us to believe that everything is spiritual. Turns out that you were right all along. To my grandparents, Dr. Gene and Betty Rice, we walk the trail that you blazed for our whole clan.

Acknowledgments

Finally, to Dr. Don Bowdle, who made me want to know God with every sinew of my mind, may you rest in peace.

Introduction
Snellville

***

Tired, blotchy, alive, her face. Hers is one of those faces you can't imagine was ever younger; her cheeks are sunken, her skin has a grayish hue, the color of cadavers. Not quite elderly but beyond middle age, she has lived so much. She doesn't smile, and her countenance suggests that inexpressible line between joy and fallenness—or someone who has discovered that perhaps the line doesn't exist.

She is my first burning memory of church, in what was then a small town called Snellville just short of the North Georgia mountains. I don't recall what brought her to the altar that night, just her walking back and forth for what seemed like an hour and praying out loud like she owned the place. She looked straight ahead while she prayed, like she was giving a stump speech, trying to convince God to vote the right way.

For that matter, the whole church at Snellville shouted at God like that, in an exuberant frenzy that was at the same time frightening and exhilarating. I don't have any mental picture of the pastor preaching behind the pulpit, just him running up the aisle from the back to the front, microphone cocked to the side of his mouth, hollering like a Rebel soldier. In my memory he looked just like Mike Ditka, but perhaps this was a later mental association. Ditka later made me nervous.

My dad took me to Snellville because he was a denominational leader who visited various congregations in our state, and he tells me that I stood on the pews with my eyes wide like I did when he took me to see David Copperfield live. But David Copperfield was sophisticated and didn't shout at the walls uncontrollably. I didn't understand him or Snellville, but I liked him better. I knew he did tricks. It looked real, but it wasn't.

At Snellville, however, the opposite was true. It looked like nonsense, but it was as real as pain. There was no other explanation for such chaos, and perhaps this is unknowingly what scared me—the fact that it couldn't be as fake as I wanted it to be. For half my childhood, my dad threatened to take me back to Snellville. I didn't think it was funny. I didn't want to be like those people.

My second earliest memories of church were the annual camp meetings that our denomination sponsored. They took place just outside of Atlanta, but people came from all over the state. They were like Snellville on steroids, but I didn't mind them as much. They say there is safety in numbers, so perhaps the couple of thousand people who showed up legitimated the experience for me.

The camp meetings were held in a concrete, open-air structure, built in the middle of a rustic campground. We called the slab with a roof "The Tabernacle," after the tent of God's presence in the book of Exodus. Only it wasn't filled so much with the cloud of God's glory as with dust and haze from the Georgia heat.

Camp meeting always took place in June or July when it was hot as all blazes, and the massive roof never could contain the overflow crowds, so they set up lawn chairs like a tailgate party on the grass outside. If it rained we just all crammed in, which made little difference in the syrupy humidity.

I remember my feet dangling off the metal folding chair as the camp meeting music climbed to its climax, changing keys when everyone expected yet bringing the crowd to its feet nonetheless. The preacher was hardly ever introduced. He worked straight from the musical crescendo to keep the train rolling toward the altar call at the end, which typically lasted longer than the sermon anyway, with the ministers huddling like football players and "tarrying," which is another word for waiting around for something to happen. And if it didn't happen that night, there wasn't much to worry about. These things lasted a week or so, with three or four services a day. If you tarried long enough, you would get your blessing.

These are all good and pleasant memories, a museum full.

This was the church as I knew it and the only church I knew. When a fifth-grade classmate asked me my religion, I had no idea what to say beyond

"Christian," which is not what he meant. He wanted a denomination, and I had heard of them, but I wasn't sure they were actually Christian. Us? We were Pentecostals. Was that a denomination?

Years later I realized that the terms weren't mutually exclusive, and I had been a part of a Pentecostal denomination from birth: the aptly named Church of God. One of our early hymns, frequently sung when new members were received into a congregation, declared,

> The Church of God is right.
>
> *Hallelujah to the Lamb!*
>
> We'll soon be dressed in white.
>
> *Hallelujah to the Lamb!*

I don't imagine that I could sing that song with a straight face today, but there is more happening in those lines than sheer arrogance. "There is one thing that is infinitely more absurd and unpractical than burning a man for his philosophy," G. K. Chesterton wrote. "This is the habit of saying his philosophy does not matter."[1] The Church of God, like any successful anybody, thought our view of the universe mattered.

The stories of the Pentecostal church that I have to tell make us seem playful. But make no mistake, we didn't show up to play, and we aren't docile. We showed up to take over the world, and we are well on our way.

Near the turn of the twentieth century, when Pentecostal Christianity exploded onto the scene of American religion, there were a few thousand Pentecostals, derided and persecuted by most anyone paying attention, be they newspapers or other church groups. We continued to grow on the margins of society until we virtually owned them. Somehow, we Pentecostals seemed to find the wrong side of the tracks everywhere we went, and we found ways to right them. We started orphanages, literacy schools, agencies dedicated to the poor and destitute. But most of all, we started churches: small, exuberant, raw churches. Something in the veins of our movement seemed to spawn them like viruses. Fast-forward to today, and the Pentecostal virus has infected the entire world.

According to Dr. Harvey Cox at Harvard University, Pentecostal Christianity represents the fastest-growing faith movement that the world

---

1. Chesterton, *Heretics*, 2.

has ever seen. An authoritative study by the prestigious Pew Forum in 2011 confirms this picture. According to the latest research, there are now approximately six hundred million of us, comprising more than a quarter of Christendom. Leaving Christendom out of the stats, that's almost one out of ten persons alive today identifying as Pentecostal! We have organized ourselves into more than seven hundred recognizable denominations, but the unorganized, nondenominational Pentecostal churches are as uncountable as the stars. We are incredibly diverse. As David Barrett describes global Pentecostalism,

> Some 29 percent of all members worldwide are white, 71 percent are nonwhite. Members are more urban than rural, more female than male, more Third World (66 percent) than Western, more impoverished (87 percent) than affluent, more family-oriented than individualistic, and, on average, younger than eighteen.[2]

If you throw a stone into a sea of the world's Pentecostals, you will most likely hit a poor woman from Africa before it ricochets to a laborer in the slums of Brazil. We are a people's church, a poor man's Spirit-religion.

Yet our strength is seen not only in the distinctiveness of our tribe. Our influence is equally seen in the virtual "Pentecostalization" of all kinds of Christian groups. Lots of Southern Baptists raise their hands in worship services now. Lots of Catholics speak in tongues (including the late Pope John Paul II!). Lots of Presbyterians pray for physical healings to occur. All of these supposed non-Pentecostals got all that from us.

Do you know a Pentecostal? If you do, you know that you do. We're the ones who, with the zeal of Mormons on bicycles, do all we can to get you into our churches. We're the ones who, if we do get you to church, scare you half to death by crying out in tongues in the middle of the hymn. We're the ones who, if you mention you have a need in the grocery store, pray for you right on the spot. We're the ones who pray quite loudly for you right on the spot if your need is of a physical nature. God may not be deaf, but we don't think He's shy, either. Like the good people of Snellville, we'll shout at Him until something happens.

---

2. Barrett, "Statistics, Global," 811, cited in Goheen, *Introducing Christian Mission Today*, 184.

I hope you are reading for one of two reasons. Perhaps you are an interested outsider who wants to know more. I'm almost inclined to point you to other resources that cover all the introductory bases in an easy-to-read format: our theological tenets, our demographics, our history. But is any group of people defined, really defined, by Wikipedia? This is a book of stories, my stories, Pentecostal stories, dirty and randomized. Maybe it is the stories, not the statistics, that will tell you everything you need to know.

Or perhaps you are reading for the same reason that I am writing: you are a Pentecostal trying to come to grips with what it means to be Pentecostal. I have been on this journey my entire life, sometimes distancing myself from these roots, other times denying them, still other times cursing them like St. Peter at the fire of Christ's trial. I have gazed upon the idols of modernity, trendiness, and stature. I have lusted after their wares. But when Pentecostalism is in your blood, there is no bloodletting. It's more like an ethnicity than a religion.

This is a book about Pentecostalism: Pentecostal theology, spirituality, and practice. Mostly, it is a book about the Pentecostal church, because we Pentecostals never have had any sense of theology, spirituality, and practice outside the nitty-gritty realities of life together in the local church. It is not meant to be comprehensive; I leave the systematic work to the experts. But it is a book in which I try to capture those major pillars of Pentecostal expression through my own experience of Pentecostalism. In that sense, it is a memoir. But I expect that all writing, somewhere down the line, is essentially memoir.

A book about Pentecostalism would be irresponsible without including its dark sides. I assume that dark sides and blind spots are part and parcel of any faith movement, so I do not shy away from discussing them. The great Southern novelist Flannery O'Connor referred to "the Christ-haunted South" as the setting for her wildly violent and dysfunctional families. Given the influence that my particular Pentecostal denomination has had on the Southern states since O'Connor passed on, we might now call the South "Spirit-haunted," and just as it does in her novels, plenty of Southern darkness has bled in. We Pentecostals have upheld blatant racism, closed-minded fundamentalism, authoritarian patriarchalism, and individualistic, gun-slinging pride. We have had our share of public debacles, moral fallouts, and leadership catastrophes. But painting the entire movement with these brush strokes alone is like denying the goodness of Mother Theresa just because the Crusades happened or a few of the popes had mistresses. The logic of that (and it is common) should actually be inverted. We know that the Crusades were stupid because of the saints that the Church has produced. We only know darkness exists because there is so much light in God's world threatening to drown it all out.

It would therefore be equally tragic to speak of darkness and not light. Too many memoirs of Christian experience, especially "conservative" Christian experience, have focused purely on darkness. These are so unoriginal. To my delight, when I crept into the attic of my Pentecostal heritage, I discovered that the room was warmly lit and filled with joy. When I tried on the musty clothes of my forbears, I found that they fit quite well.

This book is a walk up to the attic. So help me open the boxes, shake off the dust, and try them on for yourself.

"But God hath chosen the foolish things of the world to confound the wise," St. Paul says in 1 Corinthians. "And God hath chosen the weak things of the world to confound the things which are mighty; and base things of the world, and things which are despised, hath God chosen, yea, and things which are not, to bring to nought things that are" (1:27–28). The foolish, the weak, the base, the lowly—the gospel proclamation is that these are the chosen ones. That was what was going on in Snellville, and it is still going on in similar places around the world today. Go with me there, stand wide-eyed on the pews, feel the heat of the Spirit, and let's see what all the hubbub is really about.

I

The Jewish Centaur

You must learn to look at the world twice if you wish to see all there is to see.

—JAMAKE HIGHWATER

It was my second semester teaching college freshmen as an adjunct professor at our Pentecostal denomination's flagship university. The class, an introduction to the New Testament, is a core requirement for all students. One of my classroom routines is to try to understand the theological background of the students, not only for my own sake but also to guide them toward understanding the impact that context, especially social location, has on reading the New Testament. I read the Bible as a middle-class white male. I can't help it. Helping students become a bit more aware of their own lenses is an important part of a college level Bible class.

I have now taught for four semesters, and the theological breakdown of the students has been the same each time. The vast majority of them have been steeped in church from birth. This being the South, usually half of them are Baptists and the other half Pentecostals. Not many of them have read the Bible much, which is a new development in both movements, but they know the stories. These are church kids. They cut their teeth on varnished oak pews.

The fact that they are church kids actually makes the class difficult to teach. Growing up in the Southern church is a totalitarian experience. These college students have been bequeathed a complete worldview that accounts for everything: how creation was created, why we exist, what we are here to do, and how it will all wrap up one day. Church isn't one component of life. Church is the bank of raw thought material that equals life. Church equals life equals reality. Some of these kids have never been to Atlanta, let alone Paris. Peeling back the onion of their reality to get at the lenses and biases they bring to the task of biblical interpretation is no easy task. They have never considered life outside the onion. This is not a bad thing, depending on the onion.

I always begin the class by asking the students to reflect on elements in American culture that call us Christians to know something about the origins, composition, and contents of the New Testament. This is a less threatening way to move them toward considering the complexities involved in interpreting the Bible. But even this got nowhere with the students in my second semester. They have just never thought about it. If your subconscious soup has been formed by the biblical narrative, the world easily conforms to your unquestioned worldview. The church is the only culture they have known, so the thought of engaging another arena of culture is foreign. It's not that they aren't aware that nonchurch culture exists; it just gets folded into the meaning of the church in the first place. We are right and anyone else is wrong. End of discussion.

This dynamic is tricky to manage in the initial sessions of the class when we walk through the composition of the gospels. Most Christians are trained to read the Bible like the Koran or the Book of Mormon, as if it floated down from heaven on golden plates, chiseled by God like the Ten Commandments. In fact, our Bible sets Christians apart from adherents of other faiths, not only in its competing truth claims but also in the complexity of its composition. It is very careful surgery to help these students understand that what they often call "the worda God" was written by particular authors, in particular places and times, to address the particular needs of their audiences. Jesus was not a phantom floating six inches off the ground. He was a man with body odor and real theological opinions, in conversation with other Jewish teachers with body odor and real theological opinions. It may sound basic, but this is all new to the college freshmen I teach—or try to.

The crowning moment of my second semester of teaching occurred when we reached the session on the Gospel of Mark. Mark is the first narrative about the life of Jesus ever written down, so there is a lot to cover. One of the first and foremost questions that I address is the identity of Mark's audience. What we can know about this is key to determining Mark's goals and purpose. Who is Mark written to, and how do we know?

Allow me to re-create the scene:

"Determining the audience of Mark starts with determining who the first Christians were. We know that Jesus and his early followers were Jewish, so we might expect that the earliest Gospel was written for Jews. However, this is not the case. In fact, there are clear indicators in the text of Mark that the Gospel has been crafted for a Gentile Roman audience."

After pausing to ensure the students know the difference between a Jew and a Gentile, I build on the foundation I have laid, feeling confident.

"We could look at many examples in the stories of Mark that suggest this Gentile Roman audience, but the greatest example is actually the climax of the entire story. It is an alarm bell, alerting us to Mark's audience. Go ahead and turn to the end of the story, Mark 15, and we will have a look at the climax of Mark's story arc. This is, of course, the chapter that narrates Jesus's crucifixion, the moment in the early Jesus movement when it looked like the movement was over. However, when it looks as if the story is over, suddenly the least likely voice takes center stage in the narrative."

> And when the centurion, who stood there in front of Jesus, saw how he died, he said, "Surely this man was the Son of God!" (Mark 15:39)

I'm getting something in between nods and blank stares from my students. This is all so new to them. I double down on the significance of this verse.

"Even before the resurrection, this moment in Mark 15 represents the culmination of Mark's entire Gospel. Mark lays out the trajectory of the story in the first sentence of the entire book, announcing, 'The beginning of the gospel about Jesus . . . the Son of God.' As a master storyteller, however, Mark makes it difficult to track the evidence for this thesis. No one seems to discern the identity of Jesus in Mark's gospel, whether friend or foe. When Peter finally hits the nail on the head in his monumental confession of Mark 8:29, 'You are the Christ,' Jesus doesn't answer a thing, except to tell them all to shut up about it. In the next scene, Jesus calls the guy who just called him the Christ, the devil himself!"

Are they with me? I thought so a moment ago, but now it is hard to tell. Fewer nods. Blanker stares.

"It is only when the centurion confesses to the corpses on the cross, 'Surely this man was the Son of God!' that the story comes full circle. The proclamation rings out, with no one now to demand silence. Mark has proven his point. The grand reveal is that it is not the disciples, the Pharisees, or the crowds who figure out the riddle of Jesus's identity. *It is the centurion who supervised his crucifixion!* Isn't that astounding?!"

At this point in the lecture, I'm breaking for the end zone like a running back who's just stiff-armed the safety.

"So now that you know all this, why do we then assume that Mark is writing to a Roman audience?"

Crickets.

I regroup, trying to remain positive.

"We know Mark is writing to a Gentile audience because of the centurion's proclamation."

It feels like playing peekaboo with a group of children. I'm not leading them anymore. I'm trying to give them the answer to the question.

Then I unforgivably break the cardinal law of teaching. I publicly ask a question that I thought was rhetorical to students who haven't the foggiest notion what I'm talking about.

"The centurion's proclamation is so significant because of his ethnicity. Because is the centurion Roman or Jewish?"

The lone senior in the class (an education major) confidently responds. "Jewish," she announces to the class with great emphasis, as if pronouncing the winning word in a spelling bee.

My composure is withering as I try neither to embarrass her nor to capitulate to the fact that this lecture is a disaster.

"Well, no, he's actually a Gentile, because . . . as I've been saying . . . he represents the crescendo of Mark's narrative that is crafted for a Gentile audience. So we know that he is a Gentile because he is a centurion."

Then, like a gambler getting destroyed by the house, trying to make up lost ground, I go all in.

"What would you compare a centurion to in our day? Does anyone know what a centurion is?"

I throw out some options: police officer, military personnel. Nothing doing. Finally, a voice speaks clearly from the middle of the classroom. "Oh, I know. It's a half-man, half-horse."

A centaur. A Jewish centaur. And that student was not joking in the least.

I have never taken drugs, but the feeling that wafted over me when that student spoke those fateful words must approximate the experience. There was a rush of panic at the realization that I am a complete failure at my chosen vocation and should never again be allowed to professionally interact with another college student, mixed with the pure elation of having just been confronted by such an image. "And when the centaur, who stood there in front of Jesus, saw how he died, he said, 'Surely this man was the Son of God!'" Dear heaven, that is the most disturbing, most delightful thing I've ever heard. "Neigh."

In a moment, the contemporary landscape of New Testament theology flashed before my eyes. The centaurs were suddenly everywhere. One is commended by Jesus for his "great faith" in the Synoptic Gospels. Cornelius the centaur is the hinge of the book of Acts, launching the church into its Gentile mission in chapter 10. Paul the Apostle appeals to them left and right. "As they stretched him out to flog him, Paul said to the centaur standing there, 'Is it legal for you to flog a Roman citizen?'" (Acts 22:25). How might theologians handle this groundbreaking discovery?

At first I was dismayed by what I perceived to be a lack of biblical and historical literacy. Clearly falling apart now in front of a class of freshmen, who shuffled in their seats and eyed me like a specimen in a lab to see what I would say, my first instinct was to wonder if the windows were locked. I blurted out something about the existence of centaurs being historically problematic. At the same time, I tried not to pee my pants. Apparently, there is not a sharp line of differentiation anymore between *The Lord of the Rings* and the Bible. Youngsters today!

As I have reflected on this classroom experience at my Pentecostal university, however, I have come to realize that there was a lot more biblical literacy in play that day than I first imagined. In the past, if you had asked me what we Pentecostals believe, I would have run through our basic doctrinal positions: we believe in the authority of the Bible, eternal salvation through the death and resurrection of Jesus, that all the gifts of the Holy

Spirit are at work in the church today, etc. Nowadays, however, I'm more inclined to just say that we Pentecostals believe in centaurs.

Here is what I mean:

In 1918, the famous German sociologist Max Weber delivered a lecture at the University of Munich titled "Science as a Vocation," in which he said, in effect, "If you want to be a part of the modern world, grow up and bear the burden of disenchantment."[1] By that he meant that the forward march of modernity had overtaken the mystical, the magical, the spiritual, the supernatural. In the words of Madonna, "We are living in a material world," and that is all there is. Centaurs have never existed, of course, because we have no fossils of a man-horse hybrid.

But that humanity could have known then the significance of Weber's apocalyptic announcement! We now live in its aftershocks: another world war (provoked by Weber's nation, of course), the Holocaust, the nuclear bomb, the isolating power of technology, the elevation of material science to explain every beautiful mystery of creation and our shared humanity. Weber was right. The world has indeed been disenchanted, and much of religion with it.

Thank goodness that Pentecostals never bought that storyline. What do we believe? A lot of things. But all of our beliefs spring from one well: the belief that the world is as enchanted by God as it was when centaurs roamed the earth, piping on their pan flutes. It's not that we believe in the supernatural, as if it is some separate category pitted against the natural. The so-called supernatural is actually supernormal. We are, to use the term coined by sociologist Margaret Poloma, "Main Street mystics."[2]

Growing up Pentecostal, stories of the enchantment of the world were as common as weather forecasts. We never thought to study the audience of the Gospel of Mark because we *were* that audience, living in the reality Mark gave to us. There was no historical disconnect, no time travel necessary. Mark's world was our world, and it was enchanted.

There were stories of healings, of course, but they were fairly routine. A Pentecostal church that didn't have a standard litany of X-rays suddenly coming up blank and limbs popping back into place might as well be Baptist. The healing stories were only where we got started.

1. Cited in Johns, "Preaching Pentecost to the Nones," 4.
2. Poloma, *Main Street Mystics*.

There were stories of people, under the ecstatic power of the Spirit, putting their infants on top of the potbelly stoves that heated sanctuaries without being burned. There were stories of angelic visitations right through the front doors of the church. A video went around our denomination that purported to show Jesus appearing in the middle of an altar call. I saw the video when I was young, and shook with fright. I can still see him today, looking dead into the camera, some otherworldly figure. There were stories of strong men, stupefied and speechless, being escorted from the worship service back to their homes, struck dumb by the things they had seen.

"Trembling and bewildered, the women went out and fled from the tomb. They said nothing to anyone, because they were afraid." Fittingly, this is the final verse of the Gospel of Mark. The resurrection of Jesus confirms what only the centurion had the guts to declare: that when it looks like the enchantment of the world is mangled up on a cross, and you yourself did the deed, God is at play, exploding onto the scene.

This is the world we Pentecostals inhabit: a supernatural world enchanted by the Spirit of God. A world that is, in the words of Hopkins, "charged with the grandeur of God." A world that is, in the words of Psalm 24:1, wholly owned by the Lord ("and the fullness thereof"). According to Pentecostal theologian Cheryl Johns, we live in a world that is not the result of Weber's mechanistic determination, but instead

> a sacramental space wherein matter and Spirit co-mingle. Bodies are filled with divine presence, and human tongues speak of the mystery of God. In this space invisible grace is transformed into visible manifestations that say clearly "God is present." People are wonder-struck with the glory of God being manifest in the midst of common people.[3]

Such a world is full of glories, full of surprises, full of mysteries that we cannot fathom. This world makes what we believe possible.

If Weber and his followers are wrong, and the world really is enchanted, then we suddenly have to question how mythical our myths are, and how real our realities. The line between them may be much thinner than we are ready to believe. Do you believe in centaurs? They certainly wouldn't be anywhere near the craziest occurrences to pop up in God's world, re-enchanted as it has been by the resurrection of Jesus.

---

3. Johns, "Preaching Pentecost to the Nones," 6.

2

The Holy Spirit

Now when grace fills the soul, that soul rejoices and smiles and dances, for it is possessed and inspired, so that to many of the unenlightened it may seem to be drunken, crazy, and beside itself. . . . For with the God-possessed not only is the soul wont to be stirred and goaded as it were into ecstasy but the body also is flushed and fiery, warmed by the overflowing joy within which passes on the sensation to the outer man, and thus many of the foolish are deceived and suppose that the sober are drunk. Though, indeed, it is true that these sober ones are drunk in a sense.

—PHILO OF ALEXANDRIA, FIRST CENTURY CE

I know, I know. It's not surprising that a book on Pentecostal spirituality should devote a chapter to the Holy Spirit. We Pentecostals basically locked the Spirit into a celebrity endorsement deal from our inception, so He's what we're known for. We figured the mainline Protestants had already cornered the Father, what with all their rather distant talk of justice and social order. We knew the Baptists had Jesus securely in their camp, since they figured out how to package eternal salvation through Christ's death better than anybody. But if you want to talk about the Holy Spirit, find yourself a bona fide Pentecostal. I can't begin to recount how many conversations I've endured after a mainline Protestant discovered I'm "one of those," and then felt obligated to talk about how they need to know more about the Holy Spirit because He hardly ever gets talked about in their tradition. They don't mean this, of course, because the Holy Spirit of the Pentecostal tradition scares them to death. They're just nice, and committed to diversity, so they make conversation about it. I know this because I've attended Presbyterian and Lutheran seminaries. I'm telling you that those liberal Protestants are breathtakingly nice. I think they've all read Dale Carnegie.

The plain fact of the matter is that we Pentecostals have just never learned to tame our divine poster boy like the mainliners and the Baptists. We can't get the Holy Spirit to just smile nicely and give us peppy sound bites that sell the Christian lifestyle to the general public, as Jesus does for the Super Bowl MVP speeches and the Baptists. Instead, the Holy Spirit makes us and most everyone around us nervous.

So in this business of the Holy Spirit, let's brush up on those analogies we once had to decipher on the SAT: the Holy Spirit is to Pentecostal Christianity what

a. The third person of the Trinity is to God

b. The shofar is to ancient Jewish warfare

c. The seizure is to the epileptic

d. All of the above

To tell you the truth, I badly want the answer to be A. That would sound smart, as a genuine theological rationale ought to sound. But Pentecostalism rarely offers rationales in the first place, much less smart-sounding ones, so like it or not we're stuck with D.

The Holy Spirit is to Pentecostal Christianity what the third person of the Trinity is to God. This statement suggests the rather self-evident truth that God could not somehow lose one-third of God's personhood and remain the same God, or even remain fully God. If the Deity can drop 33 percent of His divinity, He doesn't get the option of keeping the train rolling at two-thirds normal operating capacity. By all reasonable accounts, being God is an all-or-nothing proposition.

In the same way, Pentecostals lay claim to the Holy Spirit as the vital third of the Christian life that others tend to ignore. This claim is principally expressed in the belief in "the baptism in the Holy Spirit," an experience subsequent to salvation akin to what happened to Christians throughout the book of Acts. John the Baptist prophesied at the beginning of Jesus's ministry that he would "baptize you with the Holy Spirit" (Mark 1:8). After Jesus rises from the dead and ascends to heaven, the prophecy is fulfilled. "All of them were filled with the Holy Spirit and began to speak in other tongues as the Spirit enabled them" (Acts 2:4). The newly Spirit-filled disciples were such a spectacle that a crowd gathered. There was a split vote over what exactly was happening. "Amazed and perplexed, they asked one another, 'What does this mean?' Some, however, made fun of them and said, 'They have had too much wine'" (2:12–13).

In my upbringing, if you didn't have the wild experience of the baptism in the Holy Spirit, you weren't of much use to God. I was talking to an older pastor whose church had shruk in attendance from forty to eight over the past few years, and he lamented a local Baptist megachurch with outreach ministries all over the city, exclaiming, "Just think of what they could do if they had the Holy Ghost!" He wasn't kidding. Because of this sometimes extreme emphasis on the baptism of the Holy Spirit, we came up with some pretty dramatic means of helping the experience to happen, leading to our second analogy.

The Holy Spirit is to Pentecostal Christianity what the shofar is to ancient Jewish warfare. To make sense of this, I recall what always seemed the strangest song sung by our church choir. I heard it so much that I can remember the verses, but the chorus says it all:

> *Send it on down*
>
> *Send it on down*
>
> *Lord, let the Holy Ghost come on down*

A tall brunette used to sing the lead, starting out in first gear and shifting into overdrive in the second verse. By the end, she always quit singing and commenced to shouting a bunch of stuff about the baptism in the Holy Spirit that wasn't even in the song. Even as a kid it seemed weird to me both to call the Holy Spirit an "it" and to talk about Him as if He were a kind of impersonal package that God lobbed your way like a football. Either way, the song and those who sang it were getting at this experience of Spirit baptism, and if choir songs didn't make it happen, somebody was bound to bust out a shofar.

Since the dawn of humanity, we have played instruments as tools to entice the gods. Ancient texts from Israel, Babylon, and Akkad are full of hymns, often with notes about the proper instrumentation. You can dress up this human penchant for magical music in orchestras, cool contemporary bands, or Gregorian chants, but our musical worship makes us all voodoos. With our instruments we charm God, we harness mystery, we enter ecstasy. Pentecostals are no exception to this legacy. We just got specific about the tradition, identifying an instrument that sends it on down every time. Like the magic lyre of Orpheus on the island of Sirens, or a divine duck call, blowing the shofar sends the Spirit on down.

The shofar is a single spiral-shaped ram's horn, and when you blow properly in the small end it sounds like a cross between a sick cow and a foghorn. In Old Testament times, the outposts blew it to rouse the troops to battle, because you could hear the thing for miles around. Also, it was an agrarian culture, so people liked the sound of cattle a lot. "Grasping the torches in their left hands and holding in their right hands the shofars they were to blow, they shouted, 'A sword for the LORD and for Gideon!'" (Judg 7:20). Shofars were serious business back then.

I don't have a clue what this has to do with life today, much less the Holy Spirit, but I've been in services where the shofar was blown unannounced and everyone hooped and hollered like we were at a sporting event, but really it was more militant than that, like the Rebel yell or the running of the bulls. I once watched a guy in Indiana roam around the entire sanctuary blowing a shofar to death, like he was trying to wake the dead. He didn't know it, but in reality he was just singing the same song I experienced growing up, but taking it to another level. When you blow a shofar, you're essentially saying that the Spirit better get the heck down here now. If nothing happens, you just end up looking like an idiot sucking on a dead ram's horn.

The problem, of course, with expecting the Holy Spirit to "come down" at the toot of a shofar or by any other formula is that it transforms Him into an It, the transcendent into the momentary, the Almighty into a commodity. The preeminent Jewish philosopher Martin Buber once warned, "Woe unto the possessed who fancy that they possess God."[1] This is always a potential danger for Pentecostals.

This danger isn't anything original. Ananias, Sapphira, and Simon the Sorcerer in the book of Acts are early examples of true believers who

1. Buber, *I and Thou*, 155.

thought they could manipulate the Holy Spirit to get them a little more status in life. A bunch of women in Paul's Corinthian congregation are so empowered by their possession of the Spirit that they're literally letting their hair down and going hog-wild in the worship service, even disassociating from their husbands as a result of their new Spirit status. Yet the New Testament is clear, especially in the book of Acts, that the Holy Spirit is not one to be possessed. Ananias and Sapphira tried that trick and wound up dead in Acts 5. Simon the Sorcerer was luckier in Acts 8.

In the New Testament worldview, the Holy Spirit, far from being a possession, is thoroughly in charge and truly possesses the believer, the church, and the direction of history. It's easy to forget this in the Pentecostal church today, since we celebrate the Spirit's presence among us. The danger is that since we know He's hanging around all the time, we expect Him to jump when we want, to jolt us with something that feels good, or even to help us achieve the American dream. In fact, this is not only incongruent with the book of Acts, but isn't even in line with our own Pentecostal experience of the Spirit's power.

The Holy Spirit is to Pentecostal Christianity what the seizure is to the epileptic. The same worship service in rural Indiana that boasted the relentless shofar blower lasted almost four hours. I've heard that Roman Catholic Mass lasts just an hour or so, which would hardly be the pregame show in our tradition. It takes us a few hours to just get through the service so that the Spirit can get to moving. It was that kind of night in Indiana, with worshippers crowding the altars and being noisy. Suddenly a young woman who looked to be a teenager threw herself to the ground and began to convulse violently. This kind of thing is not all that uncommon for us, so no one paid much attention. We assumed it was the Holy Spirit, doing His work. Luckily, her mother was present. We later found out that she was an epileptic and had suffered a dangerous seizure.

When I found out about this diagnosis, it struck me as beyond bizarre that someone could have a ferocious seizure in the middle of a church service without anyone batting an eye. This was a good example of yet another reason why as a child I didn't often invite friends to church. Mine wasn't like their churches, which didn't incorporate epileptics into the liturgy. But sometimes people in my church physically shook under the power of the Spirit. I actually remember one woman in Georgia testifying about the

physical benefits of violently shaking at church. Apparently all the jookin'
and jivin' de-cramped her ailing neck. Who knew that the Holy Ghost did
chiropractic work?

Since that Indiana service, I've realized that the connection between
epileptics and their seizures really does epitomize the Pentecostal approach
to the Holy Spirit. This is peculiar, since I haven't yet met an epileptic who
takes pleasure in losing control of her physical senses to the overpowering
torment of a seizure. They can get so bad that some even swallow their
tongues, for goodness sake. In the same way, if you really get down to it, the
baptism of the Holy Spirit in the Pentecostal tradition is pretty dangerous.
I've often been unsure if I really want the Holy Ghost hanging around, since
He always appeared to make people do weird stuff that they couldn't help.

It took church history a long time, almost two thousand years, to reclaim
the experience of the baptism of the Holy Spirit in Acts 2. We look to John
Wesley for the roots of most Pentecostal theology, even more than his own
Methodist Church these days. Although seminary trained, he sought an
experience with the Spirit that would somehow validate the authenticity
of his salvation. It happened at a Moravian meeting on Aldersgate Street in
London, during a group reading of Martin Luther's preface to the Epistle to
the Romans. Wesley records in his journal,

> About a quarter before nine, while he [Luther] was describing the
> change which God works in the heart through faith in Christ, I
> felt my heart strangely warmed. I felt I did trust in Christ, Christ
> alone, for salvation; and an assurance was given me that He had
> taken away my sins, even mine, and saved me from the law of sin
> and death.

Mind you, Wesley had long been ordained as an Anglican priest, so
this wasn't a salvation experience. He already knew what he believed. This
was a second experience that became the launching pad for Wesley's mission in life. He went on to travel the equivalent of ten times around the
globe, on horseback, preaching the gospel and establishing the Methodist
Church. That strange warmth of the Spirit that came over him on Aldersgate Street never did stop burning.

That's the kind of baptism in the Holy Spirit that I want, a toned-
down, rather sophisticated feeling of assurance, without the seizures. It's
strange that we Pentecostals point back to John Wesley as the godfather of

our doctrine of Spirit baptism, because he was so tame about it. Wesley may have felt his heart strangely warmed, but the Pentecostals I know typically feel their butts strangely fired, then sometimes proceed to act like maniacs under the vigor of the thing. It doesn't end with shaking, either. An old guy named Earl in my church back in high school used to occasionally take to twirling around like a helicopter during worship time like it was the most natural thing in the world. It was like that relay game where you bend over a baseball bat and spin around until you can't stand up. On that note, it was fairly common in that same church for some to just fall flat on their backs as though dead when struck by the power of the Spirit. Between all the spinning and falling, it sometimes looked like an elementary school PE class.

Yet these are only the explainable responses to the Spirit! When folks really got fired up, truly outrageous things could happen. I heard about a denominational conference in a stadium where a guy got to running down the stairs, and when he had nowhere left to go on the top level, he just jumped clear off of the upper deck to the bottom floor and kept right on going as if hopping down a stair. Crazy stories of this kind abound in the Pentecostal tradition. Oddly enough, the Methodists didn't pick up any of this behavior from John Wesley's experience like we did.

Maybe, just maybe, I shouldn't be so surprised by such things. The first Christian sermon, in an attempt to describe the experience of the baptism of the Holy Spirit, started with a defense of its oddity. "These men are not drunk, as you suppose," Peter explains to the skeptical crowd in Acts 2:15. "It's only nine in the morning!" According to Peter, what might be called the first Christian worship service resembled a booze-fueled bachelor party.

One Sunday in Chicago I walked over to a Presbyterian church because it was close, and the text of the day was Acts 2. It is an embarrassing chapter for Presbyterians, who like things orderly and want their kids to grow up normal. The message was a tidy and nostalgic celebration of the fact that Acts 2 represents the church's glorious birthday and that we should be thankful that God sent the Holy Spirit to birth such an institution. The minister didn't mention a thing about tongue-talking, early morning racket, drunkenness, the moon turning to blood, and all the rest of the stuff that really drives the narrative of Acts 2. You can't blame the guy; it was just one of those Presbyterian stretchings of the truth in the name of helping middle-class suburbanites not get freaked out by the Bible.

But the bottom line is that Acts 2 is freaky, and behind all of the theological high-mindedness it does look like a bunch of Spirit-fueled chaos. Even if Luke does have in mind the church's birthday, I've seen a birth before, and it's far from pretty. It is a mass of seizures that grow closer together as they crescendo into sweating and screaming and searing pain until those same seizures expel the most breathtaking thing I have ever seen: new life. But to get this beautiful result, the mother doesn't just endure the seizures. She embraces them.

An epileptic, in order to get along despite his condition, also must acknowledge and embrace the reality of the seizures. So maybe it's okay that Pentecostals act like folk possessed by this untamed Holy Spirit. By embracing and acting out the exuberance—the chaos—maybe we are both acknowledging our fallenness and birthing new life. Or maybe it is within our fallenness, with all its convulsing and blowing and formulating, that God sends his new life down.

3

Holiness

If I have to sweat for it, dear God, let it be as in Your service.
I would like to be intelligently holy.

—FLANNERY O'CONNOR

My wife and I were once offered a free stay at a vacation home in a resort community on an island in the South. We attended a church while we were there, one mostly made up of wealthy folks living in their summer beach residences, and it was perfect. And I really mean perfect, like going to church at a fancy restaurant. The pastor looked like a stockbroker, didn't yell or run around, and spoke with proper grammar. The worship band sounded like a CD. They even had a curtain that opened up on the stage when the band started, like a Broadway musical. It was the kind of church anybody could be proud of attending. These were not my people.

We hadn't seen it on our way in, but when we finished our trip and drove off the island, I found my people. A small storefront, outside of the wealthy area, with a rickety white sign somebody brush-painted in black: "Holliness Church." I wanted to take a picture but thought it might be sacrilegious. You don't mess with holiness people who don't know how to spell it. They're the real deal.

John Wesley did more to shape the landscape of American Christianity than anyone else, and he centered his movement in a theology of holiness. In fact, he essentially equated the dawn of the Methodist Church with the dawn of holiness upon the American states. "I continue to dream and pray about a revival of holiness in our day," he wrote, "that moves forth in mission and creates authentic community in which each person can be unleashed through the empowerment of the Spirit to fulfill God's creational intentions."[1] These intentions are as old as the Torah. "And ye shall be holy unto me: for I the LORD am holy, and have severed you from other peoples, that yet should be mine," God says in Leviticus 20:26. That same book's constant refrain is starkly commanding: "Be holy, for I the LORD thy God am holy."

Wesley called his view of holiness "Christian perfection," believing that it was possible and necessary for Christians to pursue a state of sanctification in which sin was no longer in play. By the latter half of the nineteenth century, a full-on "holiness movement" had erupted, seeking this perfected state of being. These holiness Christians were known for their strict practice of daily spiritual disciplines, their commitment to community, and their separation from all things "worldly." Among the many social ills that they fought was alcohol. We wouldn't know the name of Al Capone without the holiness movement. They were kind of like Puritans who were out to purify the United States.

Historically, my denomination was a part of the holiness movement of the late nineteenth century even before Pentecostalism broke forth. This is an awkward family tree with two very different trunks. Even before the holy-rolling and tongue-talking got started, we were a community sideshow for our commitment to holiness, which at first glance meant staying poor, ugly, and bored. Holiness meant that beyond the obvious teetotaling on everything from soda to gum, women also refused to cut their hair or wear makeup. Judging by some of the old mezzotint photographs, just compromising on the last one might have helped their cause.

To our credit the holiness movement that became a standard pillar of Pentecostalism was actually pretty focused. These were the days of the prohibition movement, so abstaining was part of a cause to better society. Modesty was valued as healthy for children, and in our world of Lady Gaga

---

1. Cited in Sweet, *Greatest Story Never Told*, xii.

and Miley Cyrus, who can argue with that anymore? Also, my church's early minutes encouraged members to stop using tobacco not for moral reasons but for financial reasons. They thought the money would be better spent on alms for the poor. In reality, it was all kind of beautiful, a holiness that, although couched in the rhetoric of anti-most-everything, was forcibly pro-world.

As Pentecostalism grew and spread, the social holiness movement, focused on the betterment of society, became something of a distant great grandmother. Unfortunately, our focus on holiness started to shift from outward to inward, and over the decades of the mid-twentieth century we endured the deathly march from pro-world holiness to strict separatism, perhaps at times even sectarianism.

Every movement needs some identifying boundaries to separate and define insiders from outsiders, and these are never all rational, but ours started to get out of hand. Pentecostals started separating from so many things that we forgot what any of it was about. Holiness became our philosophical trump card, which is so lazy. The focus was on the separation, not so much the things separated from, so the list is incoherent. Shorts, radio, wedding bands, baseball games, golf, chocolate, dancing, cards—if you couldn't find it in Scripture, you ought not to do it, whether or not it even existed in Jesus's day. According to my denomination's first attempt at a doctrinal statement, the New Testament was "our only rule of faith and practice," so that was that.

Compared to other Christian traditions, these random holiness codes were the Pentecostal version of water baptism, in that the first thing you were supposed to do after accepting the Lord into your heart was to get right to living holy. This usually entailed throwing away a lot of things that were representative of your former life. My grandfather "got saved" on a motorcycle racing tour when he visited his uncle Tom's Pentecostal church on a Sunday night in rural Alabama. He had hardly gotten up off his knees at the altar when the old ladies ambushed him. "Don't get yourself too excited yet," they chided. "You sure ain't gonna be of too much help to nobody with that jewelry on." You'd think such legalism would have put a damper on my granddad's newfound faith, but he didn't bat an eye. Without saying a word, he took the tie clip off, dropped it into the furnace in the fellowship hall, and walked out the door. I asked him why he never thought twice about such an odd request. "Those people were happy," he said with a distant look in his crystal eyes. "I had never seen people so happy."

Unfortunately, that holy happiness degenerated to a baser form of legalism as my grandfather followed his "call to preach." Since he only bought into some of it, the family just hid their vices from the church. We'll never know, but I'd bet that almost every minister did the same. My grandfather knew a preacher across town who was known for haranguing about the evils of television. During the World Series, my granddad dropped by unannounced and caught him watching the game on the tube in the bedroom closet.

My grandfather was no hypocrite like that, but he wasn't dumb either. He bought a family pool table and put it in the basement. When guest evangelists stayed at the house, he would order the kids not to mention the table. Once, when my young uncle had a lapse, you would have thought the walls might cave in. "Brother Preacher, you shoot pool?" my uncle asked—and everything turned to slow motion, eyes darting around the room like a standoff in an old western, tumbleweed whistling across the yard. Thankfully, the ground didn't open up and swallow them all, and nobody drew a gun. "Yes, I do, boy," the guest preacher said, and shot pool with my granddad for fifty years after.

❧

Holiness started out as something beautiful but got politicized along the way, with everybody on the lookout for the holiness Gestapo, who were known to have secret agents everywhere. If you so much as ordered a Coca-Cola, you watched your back for churchpeople. You didn't wear shorts even in your own house, in case someone should see you. As recently as the 1970s, a few denominational leaders secretly threatened not to ordain any preacher who committed the sin of golf playing. It was like our own little version of the Taliban, and plenty of it holds just as true today in Pentecostal churches across the country.

I don't know what it is about the human need to enforce control by excluding as many people as possible, but it's certainly nothing knew. Jesus himself dealt with it all the time.

Marcus Borg, one of the most famous recent scholars of the gospels, has written prodigiously about Jesus's confrontation with the "politics of holiness" in first-century Palestine. He claims that before the Roman Empire enforced their brutal tax levies on the Jewish people, the Old Testament's commandment to pay the temple tithe represented the foremost way for a good Jew to identify himself as a good Jew. The Old Testament tithe was only 10 percent, after all; it was meant to be within the reach of everyone. That 10 percent paid for all kinds of things, not only the ministry of the priests but also plenty of social service programs for the poor. At the time of the tithe, before Rome tore the nation to pieces, there were no distinct religious sects within Israel.

When Jesus came on the scene, he was faced with a fragmented people who had forgotten themselves. And unfortunately, there arose many competing religious groups attempting to tell them who they were or weren't. The tithing system wasn't realistic anymore, with a lavish temple rebuilt by Herod and Roman taxes in many cases taking a third of a farmer's income, so the main question became how to distinguish a good Jew. I guess he could have chosen any group as his sparring partner, but Jesus locks in on the Pharisees and never lets go of the issue. Their answer to this question? Holiness defines a good Jew. And who defines holiness? Why the Pharisees, of course.

If you think that not allowing girls to wear pants is oppressive, you haven't seen anything. The Pharisees transformed holiness into an accounting system worthy of the IRS. They broke the Torah down into 613 commandments that could be taught orally to the illiterate masses. They had rules defining what was and was not considered work on the Sabbath. They had regulations about speaking to women in public. They had a penchant for stoning people. "From the Pharisaic point of view," Borg writes, "the most offensive of the nonobservant were said to have lost all civil and religious rights; they were deprived of the right to sit on local councils and lost their place as children of Abraham in the life of the age to come. They became 'as Gentiles.'"[2] These guys were no joke. Their motto: be holy or we will come after you.

The saddest part of it is that their characterization as the "bad guys" of the gospels is quite inaccurate. Historical Pharisaism is actually a majestic movement, one with a deeply spiritual center that, unlike the other Jewish sects of the time, survived long after the destruction of Jerusalem to become the rabbinic Judaism of the last two millennia. I suppose Jesus spent his time heckling them because he saw that beauty and hoped that the Pharisees could become their true selves.

2. Borg, *Jesus*, 89.

It wasn't that Jesus thought that the Pharisees had gone too far in their holiness codes but that they hadn't gone far enough. The Sermon on the Mount is the best example of this, since Jesus virtually laughs at their view of holiness as way too lightweight. "You have heard . . ." he tells the people over and over in Matthew 5, reciting back to them the Pharisees' favorite holiness codes. "But I tell you . . ." The Pharisees' holiness is a Nerf version of the real thing. Don't murder? Give me a break. "Anyone who is angry with his brother will be subject to judgment" (5:22). Anybody can stop just short of the deed of adultery; try eliminating lust from your thoughts. "If your right eye causes you to sin, gouge it out and throw it away" (5:29). Heck, even Moses was misunderstood on divorce, so take it off the table. "I tell you that anyone who divorces his wife, causes her to become an adulteress" (5:32). Here the Pharisees were all-consumed with holiness codes, but Jesus says to try this on for size: "Be perfect, as your heavenly father is perfect" (5:48). Be better than holy, he says. Be mature. Be complete. Be perfect. Be perfectly holy.

He was right, of course, being the Son of God and all, that holiness just doesn't work from the outside in. Better yet, he was right about the point of holiness in its entirety. To this end, the Sermon on the Mount is such a devastating leveling of the playing field before God that the very notion of spiritual elites who get to hold their own holiness over the heads of others is outlandish, as if holiness were a possession. Here the Pharisees were keeping a scorecard as if the more holy one was, the happier God was. But Jesus says that God is already happy. It's the world that's in trouble. "You are the light of the world," he says, so "let your light shine before men, that they may see your good deeds and praise your Father in heaven" (Matt 5:14, 16). The holiness of Jesus is not for the benefit of the holy or of God. Holiness is for the benefit of the world.

Before the unfortunate inward shift that led to our own silly holiness codes, Pentecostals naturally lived that kind of holiness. They built orphanages, started Bible colleges, led in Prohibition, fed the hungry, taught the illiterate to read, and served the poor. They were simple folk, of course, and probably not the best spellers. In our technological information age, it might do us some good to remember that you don't have to know how to spell to be holy, much less to be happy. And if all the rolling, dancing, and shouting were any indication, they were perfectly happy.

"No half-measures are any good," C. S. Lewis wrote of holiness. "Christ says, 'Give me all. . . . Hand over the whole natural self, all the desires which you think innocent as well as the ones you think wicked—the whole outfit. I will give you a new self instead. In fact, I will give you myself.'"[3] Jesus didn't even invent that kind of holiness. It was old as Leviticus, founded in God's challenge to "be holy, for I the LORD am holy." And just like the teachings of Jesus, the book of Leviticus champions the complete transformation of the human person into a *whole* person. *Holiness equals wholeness*; that seems to be the point. People still get bogged down in the minutiae of all the dietary laws in the Torah and miss the amazing reality of such beautifully banal commandments: God wants you to be so whole that he cares about what you eat, who you sleep with, how you worship. As modern psychology continues to slice the human personality every which way, that kind of wholeness could really make a comeback.

In the Southern writer Rick Bragg's history of his grandparents' life in rural Alabama, he recounts a conversation between his mother and grandfather when she was just a child:

> "Why is she so mad at you, Daddy?" she would ask him when she was older.
> "Well, hon," he would say, "she's a Holiness."
> "What's that?" Margaret said.
> "A Holiness," he said, "is somebody who ain't never had no fun."

What a sad commentary for all of us Pentecostals, that holiness could be rotted down to something so shallow. Yet there is also hope all around us, as the Pentecostal church is now climbing out of the rathole of colorless legalism to once again embody a holiness that isn't just separate from, but on behalf of, the world.

> Ava, he explained, sometimes forgets that she is one, and has some fun before she realizes she is having any.
> "She backslides," he explained, "which makes her tolerable."[4]

If but all of us could backslide into true "holliness."

3. Lewis, *Complete C. S. Lewis*, 157.
4. Bragg, *Ava's Man*, 136.

4

Authority

Children are still the way you were as a child, sad like that and happy—and if you think of your childhood you live among them again, among the solitary children, and the grownups are nothing, and their dignity has no value.

—RAINER MARIA RILKE

Words have a life of their own, and this is the scariest part of writing a book that is a memoir, as in the end all books are memoirs. Even though these chapters tell my story, they are not in and of themselves who I am. In proofing my own words, I have a keen sense that a persona has been created in my name, and the danger is that this persona is more the projection of who I would like to be than who I truly am. I know this is a danger because I keep catching myself exaggerating those criticisms I have of my tradition, and even grinding axes that, when it comes down to it, I really don't even care about grinding. I guess this temptation stems from the fact that being a little bit cynical is trendy and makes you sound devious and naughty. The truth is that I am neither.

The oldest son of an ordained minister who was the oldest son of an ordained minister, I became an ordained minister. I have walked the line my entire life—eager to please my parents, a good student, reluctant to significantly challenge the traditions passed down to me. This book may be about as rebellious as I've ever been, which isn't saying much. When I was in middle school I was often called a goody-goody. As weird as our church services could get, I loved going to church. Life was structured, predictable, and straight-laced. I understood how it all worked, and I played by the rules.

But—and this is a big caveat—there was always one week out of the year when the tables were turned on all of that, one week when the sky may as well have been polka-dotted like in some kind of Alice's Wonderland. As C. S. Lewis's fictional children escaped into Narnia where they were transformed into warriors and kings, our parents and church leaders annually opened a portal for us to try these new identities—and then closed it just as quickly. In the ancient Greco-Roman world, they called such a week the Saturnalia, during which the societal chains of authority were radically reversed. In my upbringing, the week was called church camp.

A while ago I noticed that a newly released documentary was creating quite a stir. I suppose any documentary that is broadly released in American theaters is a big deal, but this one was previewed on all the national news programs, including the one with Matt Lauer, who has always struck me as a jerk. It's called *Jesus Camp*, and it chronicles some Pentecostal church camp in Michigan that claims to crank out "warriors for Jesus." So I watched the film, and I felt right at home. It was like watching old family movies. I went to these kinds of camps every year when I was a kid.

Of course, the media took to bashing the things depicted in the documentary the second they heard about it, and on first blink it's hard to blame them. It does look like a bunch of kooky religious brainwashing—little children being worked up into an emotional frenzy with all of this military rhetoric: "I'm in the Lord's army," etc., etc. It seems only a short leap away from the Middle Eastern kids lifting up Kalashnikov rifles on the news ("young jihadists for Jesus"). This is the kind of summer camp I knew well, but there was much more behind it than aggressive oratory. It was about authority, pure and simple, with nothing mediating between you and God. It was serious, and it was nothing to play with, even among children.

Don't get me wrong: on the surface, our summer church camps were about as conservative as an Italian convent. Girls couldn't wear shorts, the sexes couldn't swim together ("mixed bathing," we called it), and you carried your 1611 Authorized King James Bible just about everywhere. But even with these strictures firmly in place, there was a feeling of sheer hedonism that went with that many Pentecostal kids in one place. Here were hundreds of children just like me, let loose with limited adult supervision to rule the roost for a week. There was an electrifying freedom to it all, like an upbeat, Christian version of *Lord of the Flies* without the plane crash and the social Darwinism and the pig's head on a stake.

I remember well a particular moment of anti-authoritarian debauchery. I was perhaps seven or eight years old, and the last night of camp in our dorm of about a dozen boys had quickly surged into a candy-fueled riot, with lots of leaping from bunk to bunk and running around screaming like lunatics in the middle of the night. Somehow we got word that a camp administrator was on his way to put an end to our party, and I decided right then and there to greet him by waving my naked, white butt all up in his face like a hula dancer. In a second, my bunkmates caught the fever, and that denominational official whose face I can still remember got himself quite an eyeful of a bunch of eight-year-old bottoms. The inmates had taken over the asylum, and he walked out with nothing but an empty threat to tell our parents. We weren't afraid; we had triumphed over the great Goliath.

Looking back to that incident, it was actually quite fitting for a bunch of budding Pentecostal kids to moon the authorities. After all, we've been doing it from our inception.

As a writer, what is most scary is the space between what is written and what is read. This inevitable pocket where the words are mediated is open to infinite confusion and misinterpretation. Someone may read a segment of this book and take me as a recalcitrant rebel. Another may ingest the same passage and consider me a prudish conformist. But what if I could somehow offer my experiences and my very self to you exactly as they are, by taking away your authority to mediate them? What if the space where things are argued, interpreted, and analyzed could be suddenly cut out of the mix, and no validation of my words was needed beyond the words themselves? What if we never knew a thing about the work of literary criticism? Of course none of this can be done, and so your reading of my words is governed by what you know of grammar, of propriety, of what comprises entertainment or appeal or crap. But Pentecostalism has tried its best to transcend these rules of authority, that space where certain men mediate

God's call to other men, and it has made for some really interesting arrangements. Because like it or not, you've got to fill the interpretive space with something.

The earliest adherents of our movement fought the very notion of human authority tooth and nail. This was rooted in the Azusa Street Revival, which was the tinderbox that sparked global Pentecostalism at the beginning of the twentieth century. During this revival, an illiterate black preacher named William Seymour built one of the largest churches in the world in the middle of the worst section of Los Angeles by drawing the likes of God knows who. Seymour routinely preached with an egg crate on his head so that nobody would focus on him, but who on earth wanted to? No pedigree, no training, no authority, no "legitimating power of credentialed religion," to use a term from Walter Brueggemann.[1] That kind of leader was and is a joke, and there he went inaugurating the greatest Christian movement the world has ever seen.

My denomination began similarly with an anti-establishment passion, and this more than a half century before the sixties. In fact, the earliest records of what would become the worldwide "Church of God" disqualified human structures so randomly that one wonders how in God's name a denomination ever came out of it. The first "minutes" of the first meeting of these early Pentecostal churches that was organized enough to have minutes begins by packing heat:

> We hope and trust that no person or body of people will ever use these minutes, or any part of them, as articles of faith upon which to establish a sect or denomination. . . . Our articles of faith are inspired and given us by the Holy Apostles and written in the New Testament which is our only rule of faith and practice.[2]

With nothing more than this pithy introductory statement to some notes scrawled out with little attention to grammar, two millennia of creeds, advanced theological education, and pretty much all authoritarian forms of church government were swept clean off the table.

Yet in an ironic twist, almost immediately the same folks set about establishing a denomination, with a copyrighted name, standard articles of faith (otherwise known as creeds), and as much church government as the Catholics. In fact, the leader of this first meeting was eventually elected

1. Brueggemann, *Sabbath as Resistance*, 72.
2. Synan, *Holiness-Pentecostal Tradition*, 78.

"General Overseer" of the denomination for life, just like the pope, before he was impeached and defrocked. Try as we may, "Pentecostal denomination" remains an experiment at best, an oxymoron at worst. Part of our DNA is to prize authority so purely that we inevitably undermine its centralization.

We Pentecostals like our authority on the rocks without a mixer or a chaser—pure and unfiltered, one hundred proof. This taste for unmediated authority comes through from the momentous to the mundane, from church camp to the church pew. But it only starts with summer camp. Its expression takes many forms thereafter.

I remember well the first time I got close to the most potent display of such unmediated authority—an exorcism. I had caught glimpses of this kind of thing a few times in adult church, but it was never much to write home about. This one occurred, unsurprisingly, at a weekend youth retreat called Jesus Jam, complete with all the same worshipping, shaking, and falling that is portrayed in *Jesus Camp*.

I don't recall how things got started, but several adults took a girl who was writhing around in spasms into a back room, and I wasn't going to miss it. I peered through the window as one country guy with bad teeth took the lead screaming back and forth with the girl, explaining that there wasn't a chance in hell he was going to have any conversation with a demon and if it knew what was good for it then it would leave the girl that instant. Since then, I've seen some exorcisms on television news shows, and they get pretty elaborate. There are scripted prayers and icons and crosses and chanting and incense and such. But in that back room I got a look into a kind of authority without trappings, as that country boy talked to that demon like it was a six-year-old child. And wouldn't you know it, the thing raised a little fuss and then calmed down just as quickly. She was freed.

Paul Tillich once preached, "He who tries to be without authority tries to be like God, who alone is by Himself."[3] But what of those who lay claim to the authority of heaven and earth? "And these signs will accompany those who believe: In my name they will drive out demons; they will speak in new tongues; they will pick up snakes with their hands; and when they drink deadly poison, it will not hurt them at all; they will place their hands on sick people, and they will get well" (Mark 16:17–18).

3. Tillich, *New Being*, 85.

With that kind of authority suddenly available to whoever—illiterate black preachers, Appalachian miners, Jesus campers, and country exorcists—it's pretty easy to see how we got Christian televangelists. Because once the Pentecostal message dawns on you, that all God's power is available without any prerequisites, who is going to stop you from doing or saying whatever you want, or whatever you subjectively interpret the Spirit to be doing or saying? If you can essentially moon demonic authorities, then you've got the right to moon whoever else. Since both are quite entertaining, Christian television stations pump out unmediated authority twenty-four hours a day, telling you that you're not rich because you haven't rebuked enough demons, and generally annihilating anything that reeks of structure, much less denominationalism. And who can tell half of these wackos that they're wrong? Many of them have stripped even the Bible out of the mix, so that not even a sacred text mediates between them and God. With that kind of authority, and all the prosperity preaching, it's not hard to see why televangelists are so popular.

For most Pentecostals, however, unmediated authority plays out on the much more mundane side of the spectrum, summarized in the infamous statement "God told me to." I suppose it was St. Paul who first came up with this idea, since he made it clear that he was an apostle regardless of never being one of the Twelve, much less having spent any legitimate time with Jesus (heavenly visions didn't count as much; see Galatians 1). And even though Paul wasn't much of a speaker, he damned those who disagreed with him because God had called him to do what he was doing and that was that. "And I will keep on doing what I am doing in order to cut the ground from under those who want an opportunity to be considered equal with us in the things they boast about" (2 Cor 11:12). Them sound like fightin' words to me.

It is quite a trump card, "God told me to," something that is hard to argue with. At my Pentecostal college, it was the line of choice in difficult breakups. I vowed not to use it, of course, since blaming the fact that I found a prettier girlfriend on God seemed rather sacrilegious, but once you get started it's hard to stop. The phrase is a cure-all. It so quickly and easily ceases the conversation—"God told me to"—and ceases it in such a way that gives you the moral high ground forever. Because to rebut such a claim means either to deny God or to deny the other's connection to God, which in Pentecostal circles are close to the same thing anyway. Better just to stand there in embarrassment. Who are you to decide what God told me to do? "God told me to break up with you." End of story, conversation, and relationship.

And of course, this is the question that Pentecostals have been asking all these years, whether they ever knew it or not. "Who are you? Who really are you?" Beyond the fancy titles, prestigious degrees, and lofty positions, who are you? If all of these props that we set up before God to protect Him from all of our humanness were instantly eradicated, what of you is left? And if this is the you that matters, the real you, aren't we all painfully equal? And if we are painfully equal, the floodgates have been opened for any old person to play a part, to be a hero, to cast out devils, to deeply know God.

"And having disarmed the powers and authorities, he made a public spectacle of them, triumphing over them by the cross," Paul says in Colossians 2:15, because what looked like the cruelest of human instruments became instead the instrument of God's victory—the place where God turned the tables on all that had been in authority before. The nakedness of Jesus all mangled up on the tree was the spectacle, of course, the very soul of God laid bare. So I guess to be a Pentecostal is to live your life as an extension of God's nakedness, turning the tables on those same powers and authorities. And if some innocent bystanders happen to get mooned along the way, perhaps like the centaur who gambled for Jesus's clothes, they too can still catch a glimpse of God's glory.

5

Culture

The church doesn't have a social strategy, the church is a social strategy.

—STANLEY HAUERWAS AND WILL WILLIMON

When I began working at a large Pentecostal church that is historically considered one of the most progressive in our denomination, I suggested a simple community outreach idea: an Easter egg hunt. The custom of gathering eggs at Easter time goes back to the Protestant Reformation more than five centuries ago, and all sorts of churches host them now. Parents will go nuts over watching their kids bumble about on the grass, so egg hunts function as palatable community events that make Christians seem more neighborly and less "religious." They are like those old Mormon commercials, humanizing us. "See, we aren't that much different from you. We dye eggs!"

I was ready to bring my bold outreach idea to the big stage of our community. "An Easter egg hunt is low-hanging fruit during this time of year!" I exclaimed to our church staff. "Imagine the crowd we could draw from the surrounding neighborhoods! It will be a great way to reach potential visitors!" Instantly, my enthusiasm chased back into my throat. I felt the oxygen sucked out of the room, the potted plant on the credenza withering.

Our children's minister's voice cracked as she almost began to cry. In flirting with Easter eggs, which are nowhere in the Bible, she explained, I had mixed darkness and light. In reality, I had crossed the deadly Pentecostal line, the culture line, the line between us and "the world."

I knew this line well from my youth. "The world" was routinely condemned as the domain of Satan. As a child, I was once reprimanded at a Christian camp for singing the chorus of "Ghostbusters." If it's "secular," it's "worldly." During that same camp, there was a sermon about the evils of Michael Jackson, especially relevant since he was in the middle of taking the 1980s by storm. The preacher was especially horrified by the now classic anthem "Bad," which seemed to her like moral vertigo. "I'm bad!" the king of pop proclaimed, moonwalking his way to the top of the charts. "Woe to those who call evil good and good evil," she carped, quoting Isaiah 5:20. "It's all worldly," she concluded. "Michael Jackson is of *the world*," this last word drawn out slowly, like she was telling a ghost story.

"Avoid the very appearance of evil," Paul said in 1 Thessalonians 5:22, but a more explicit list of said appearances of evil sure would have helped. There is a lot of wiggle room in "the very appearance," so I grew up wildly navigating this line between God and "the world." My friends and I bought secular cassettes, liked them, went to youth group, felt guilty, and staged spectacles where we smashed them to smithereens with the zeal of fascists at a book burning. Then the buzz wore off, and the "very appearance of evil" line felt like it had moved. So we bought the same albums again. Record companies loved us.

Holding hands with my girlfriend didn't seem to appear evil at all, but what after that? Interlocked-finger handholding? Hugging? Kissing? What kind? "Avoid the very appearance"—it could all seem so gray. I heard a hundred messages answering the ultimate dating question for Christian teenagers: "How far is too far?" This was a pressing question to Pentecostal young people, and the Bible didn't say a specific thing about it!

And so we navigated this fuzzy culture line, attempting to stay on the right side, avoiding "the world" and "the very appearance of evil." Michael Jackson, kissing girls, Santa Claus ("Just switch the letters around and it spells 'Satan'—the devil invented Santa to take Christ out of Christmas!"), every such dilemma both a conundrum and a call to arms. Will we be true to our faith, or will we compromise to the culture of this world?

This navigation is more tenuous as an adult. In our church, the conversation about the egg hunt that led to tears also led to some really fascinating dances around the culture line. The hardliners would no sooner endorse an egg hunt on the church lawn than they would lay out little flaming penta-grams for children to collect in baskets. The progressives around the table were a bit more nuanced. They were fine with the egg hunt as long as there was no trace of the Easter bunny. I think the story goes that the Easter bunny lays the Easter eggs, so this strikes me as a strange place to draw the culture line. I guess we could make up our own myth, should the chil-dren ask the question: "The resurrected Jesus put out the eggs." That would match up with the holiday nicely, and it might satisfy the hardliners too.

What is really strange is that this same church where I proposed the egg hunt produced a "Halloween alternative" every year for two straight decades. The event was huge; more than a thousand children showed up. There was candy, costumes, games, and trickery. The key difference is that the church didn't call it a Halloween party; they called it a Harvest Festival. And the children were allowed to dress up only as Bible characters or ani-mals. No witches, goblins, or vampires could enter; they would be turned away at the gates. The whole scene must have looked like a giant movie set of Noah's ark . . . without the ark. Halloween was evil, so we were saving people from it, giving them an alternative. But does the absence of ghouls mean no homage is paid to Halloween?

These are all examples of our navigation of culture. Like a line in the middle of the highway, we Pentecostals swerve all around it, flee from it, straddle it. We certainly don't stay in our lane, allowing culture to pleasantly drive us down the road. We are not often sure where we stand in relation-ship to culture, and we don't need to be. When push comes to shove, we'll just create our own culture at the drop of a hat.

Our twisted relationship with culture goes back a way, stemming from what is now called the fundamentalist movement of the 1920s. Before this, Pen-tecostals were weird, but we were never accused of being separatist jerks about it. We were so committed to caring for the poor and the outcasts in our early days that a vital integration with culture was natural. We spurned booze, Hollywood, and nonsense, of course, but we didn't run away from anything. God was re-creating the world by His Spirit through us, for heaven's sake.

Then came the rocky marriage with fundamentalism in the 1920s that set us on a mazy path with culture. We wanted to be accepted by the broader

Christian community, so we accommodated to a bride that has not treated us well. The fundamentalist movement, which was an early theological version of today's Religious Right, arose in response to creeping liberalism in the mainline churches about a century ago. In the face of liberal theological trends associated with Harvard and other Ivy League universities, a group of conservatives churned out scores of pamphlets outlining the "fundamentals" of the Christian faith: the inerrancy of the Bible, the virgin birth of Christ, His dual humanity and divinity, the substitutionary atonement of the cross, Jesus's bodily resurrection, and His imminent second coming. The pamphlets were so widespread that the name stuck; the fundamentalists became the new face of common-man Christianity.

Even though fundamentalist leaders roundly denounced Pentecostals as heretics and crazies—one notoriously called us "the last vomit of Satan," while another suggested we were "founded by a Sodomite"[1]—somehow we largely signed on to the fundamentalist worldview. Fundamentalists were tired of liberal Christians trying to earn a place in the world by sacrificing the ancient doctrines of the church in order to fit into modern culture, so they sought to draw a line in the dirt between Christians and "the world." We believe in creation. They believe in evolution. We believe in the inerrancy of the Bible. They believe it is full of myth and symbol. We believe in Christ alone. They believe in many roads to God. Everything was bifurcated, and we withdrew from culture into our shell. Or so the story goes.

The reality is that Pentecostals are decidedly not fundamentalists, although we certainly adhere to the original fundamentals. The problem is not so much with beliefs about God as it is with how we think God wants us to act toward our culture. We tried on the fundamentalists' shoes, even ran a while in them, but they never have fit. Withdrawal from the "the world" may be a part of some corners of our haggard past, but it is not the way of our future. Harvey Cox describes these growing pains:

> Within the churches, denominations, associations, schools, and publications of the pentecostal movement a sharp clash is under way between those who would like to capture it for the fundamentalist party and for the religious-political right, and those who insist that its authentic purpose is to cut through creeds and canons and bring the Gospel of God's justice and the Spirit's nearness to everyone.[2]

1. White, *When the Spirit Comes*, 41.
2. Cox, *Fire from Heaven*, 310.

Cox's summary is now a generation old, and our marriage with fundamentalism has all but disintegrated. The divorce papers between Pentecostalism and fundamentalism have been drawn up and are ready to be signed.

❧

Admittedly, some Pentecostal circles still resonate with fundamentalist tendencies. But the hangover is quickly wearing off as Pentecostals naturally assume the posture not of withdrawing from culture but *engaging* the world around us. To be engaged is to be committed, but not married. It is to overlap but remain distinct. Because we were always willing to separate ourselves from "the world," we gained a true identity. And now we are ferociously back again, a bunch of awakened giants, ready for the cultural fights that matter.

The pastor of the largest church in Europe is an African Pentecostal who ignited the movement that overthrew communism in the Ukraine. Each week, Pastor Sunday Adelaja challenges his twenty-five thousand members to pray about starting new social outreaches as a natural component of their faith. As a result, this single church has created more than three thousand nonprofit organizations and sponsored more than 140 bills in the Ukranian Parliament. Adelaja criticizes the stereotype that Pentecostals only want to talk about fundamentalist withdrawal:

> I pastor a large church, but it's not a big deal to me, and it's not my goal. It's just a platform God has given us as a group to impact our nation. . . . There is absolutely no use in having a big church without changing the culture, speaking to society, and curing social ills.[3]

Adelaja also admits to praying for weeks at a time, interrupted only by sleep. This is the face of today's Pentecostalism: engaging culture because we have found who we are.

The largest worldwide Pentecostal denomination is called the Assemblies of God, and their largest congregation in the United States is in Chicago, led by Dr. Wilfredo De Jesus, one of *Time* magazine's "100 most influential people" of 2013. The thirteen-year-old church is located on Chicago's tough West Side, and De Jesus attributes their outrageous growth to simply ministering to the marginalized and creating new conversations around matters of public policy. "I think the Church is the largest

---

3. Adelaja, *Church Shift*, 57.

institution, the greatest institution on the planet Earth," De Jesus says. "The Bible teaches us that we're the head and not the tail. Although we've been acting like the tail for so many years, this is the season for the Church to be the head, and so we're leading the way."[4]

Those are not the words of some bleeding-heart activist. This is a tongue-talking Pentecostal pastor speaking, and he is the face of today's Pentecostalism. Far from withdrawing from "the world," we are engaging culture once again, because we know who we are.

The list of examples goes on and on. From pastors to politicians, attorneys to professors to business leaders, Pentecostals are now cultural change agents around the world. Many credit Pentecostalism for the rise of democracy in the developing world, since we so naturally rally everyday people to better their societies. We continue to be champions for the plight of the poor, not from some sanitized government office space but from the gutters themselves. We aren't advocates; we are residents. Our congregations fill up the *favellas*. That is where we best live, unwithdrawn.

"For God so loved the world," the most famous verse of the Bible begins, and all kinds of Christians have struggled with such a bold announcement. It is so naked. In some ways it is easier to sympathize with earlier conceptions of God that are better suited to a fundamentalist worldview. "God said to Noah, 'I am going to put an end to all people, for the world is filled with violence because of them.'" Is this not, like the fundamentalist vision, sensible?

Of course it is. It is perfectly sensible. That's why we railed against Michael Jackson and turned Easter eggs into the forbidden fruit of Eve. That's why we veered away from the "secular" and created campy Halloween alternatives. We were trying to remain pure from Noah's world. We were trying to be sensible.

G. K. Chesterton described such sensibilities before fundamentalism systematized them: "The madman is not the man who has lost his reason. The madman is the man who has lost everything except his reason."[5]

"For God so loved the world . . ."

4. Menzie, "Pastor Wilfredo De Jesus," par. 10.
5. Chesterton, *Orthodoxy*, 11.

6

Preaching

I'm watching him from the back. He takes the text of the speech that he was reading, and he moves it to the side of the lectern. And then he grabs both sides of the lectern, and I say to the person standing next to me—whoever that was—I said, "These people don't know it, but they're about ready to go to church."

—CLARENCE JONES, SPEECHWRITER FOR DR. MARTIN LUTHER KING, JR., ON THE "I HAVE A DREAM" SPEECH, 1963

When I graduated from a Presbyterian seminary, it felt like the green jacket presentation of the Masters golf tournament. I had actually made it: the lone Pentecostal in a sea of smart, affluent Presbyterians. Sometimes it seemed like going to graduate school in an F. Scott Fitzgerald novel, sans the sexual escapades. The refined way people talked to one another, the wine, the lefty politics.

My Pentecostal family was there with me, of course, all dolled up. And all the Presbyterian families gathered, looking like they might break out the lawn croquet and white tails at any moment. I didn't care if I was out of place. I earned the diploma like everyone else. And I was ready to soirée it all up at graduation.

The commencement preacher approached the lectern. There was a pregnant pause. I thought a gospel choir might emerge out of nowhere. I could hear Handel's Hallelujah Chorus wanting to erupt from the cathedral walls. We had all made it through and the excitement was palpable.

In Pentecostal circles, this kind of energy would be channeled into a sermon that would peel the paint off the walls. I was ready. The preacher looked at us. I assumed he was just revving the engine, harnessing energy that would explode into a jubilant sermon. I waited on him to strip his jacket off and go to town.

Instead, when he was finished looking around the room and pausing, the Presbyterian preacher put on his glasses and read his manuscripted notes right from the page. "God will do His work with you and without you," I remember him saying in monotone. He barely looked up, and he never raised his voice. This was our rousing call to go preach the gospel unto all nations.

He was preaching in the Presbyterian tradition, of course. But this kind of preaching was so foreign to me that I felt oddly embarrassed, both for him and for me, as I sat in my cap and gown. I felt blushed but I did not know why.

A little-known fact about global Pentecostalism is that we build our faith communities around the centerpiece of preaching. A lot of people fail to realize this because it's our spiritual fireworks that tend to get noticed and make our movement distinctive, not our sermons. But this outlook is mistaken. The Jews have often been called the People of the Book. We Pentecostals might be called the People of the Preacher.

It was Martin Luther who introduced preaching as the centerpiece of Christian worship during the Protestant Reformation of the sixteenth century, with his emphasis on *sola scriptura* (Scripture alone) as the proper foundation of the true faith. Still, the difference between a Lutheran worship service and a Catholic Mass is not immediately apparent today. Although a radical, Luther held on to a bunch of the Roman Church's accoutrements: a high view of the sacraments, rote prayers of call and response, goblets, robes, glumness, lectionaries, glum paint, manuscript sermons. Pentecostals, for better or worse, dispensed with all these things. If there is a Hammond organ and a preacher, church can be had. I once worked at one of the largest Pentecostal churches in Atlanta, with a huge staff and a fancy new building. My pastor used to say, "We don't need this building. Just put me and the music director in the parking lot and they'll come." He was probably right. You might say we have always held on to the "protest" in Protestantism with greater extremity than Martin Luther.

As a result, it is practically a truism to say that Pentecostal preachers go all out. If you are not a Pentecostal, you cannot imagine the things that I have seen.

There is the sheer decibel level of our preaching, of course. Many of our preachers do not believe that preaching is preaching if the sermon is not shouted at the top of the lungs from start to finish, always into a microphone. I have heard preachers in tiny sanctuaries with a few dozen people, and they still use the microphone. The heightened decibel level is often said to be that which distinguishes preaching from "teaching." It's perfectly fine if you aren't screaming; you're just teaching, and we value that too. But if you claim to be preaching, then you'd better bring the heat.

There is the athletic nature of Pentecostal preaching as well. In our tradition, preaching can take a toll on the body. Some of our guys carry a towel on their shoulder throughout the sermon, like a heavyweight boxing coach, just to keep the sweat out of their eyes. I've seen our preachers sweat through double-breasted suits like they were undershirts, royal blue jackets deepening to midnight navy by the time of the altar call. Our preaching calisthenics are myriad: jumping, dancing, running, crying. Sometimes we create impromptu skits by pulling people from the congregation, like a comedy sketch show. It's weird that so many of our preachers struggle with their weight, given the calories they burn up there. "Whose line is it anyway?"

There is the dialogical nature of Pentecostal preaching, often associated with African-American Christianity but normative for Pentecostals everywhere. I was in Haiti once, teaching pastors at a Pentecostal seminary, and I was immediately taken aback by the intensity of the questions routinely shot at me from the class. It seemed to me that the students were sparring with me rather than creating discussion (my translator referred to the experience as the "shooting range," which didn't help things). After I adjusted to the new scene, I realized that the Haitians were just living out their Pentecostalism in the classroom. Since our movement eschews experts, truth must emerge from dialogue. I was a preacher to them, not a PhD, so interruption was the ultimate compliment. In this regard, Pentecostal sermons may be more like rabbinic conversations than anything else.

But perhaps what is most fun about Pentecostal preaching is that it is dramatically improvisational. Our sermons typically have a destination, but we hew the road out in real time, with all kinds of unexpected stops along the way. It is nothing like the Presbyterian seminary preacher from my graduation. We are suspicious about pulpit notes in general, but a full manuscript is virtually sacrilege. "If you tell the truth," Mark Twain said, "you don't have to remember anything."[1]

All these characteristics form the outer shell of Pentecostal preaching. What are its contents? The answers are simple: Pentecostal preaching is rooted in narrative and forwarded as testimony.

Historically, Pentecostal preaching has been steeped in the narratives, or stories, of the Bible and of common life. In Pentecostal sermons, it isn't that something is being taught. That is for the Sunday school hour. Instead, something is being vehemently agreed upon. And that something is not a bullet point, not a proposition, but a raw happening—a terribly human experience of pain, of deliverance, of life, of God. What is being agreed upon is a narrative.

Steven Land of the Pentecostal Theological Seminary emphasizes this focus on narrative in his description of the manner in which early Pentecostal sermons lived into the stories of the Bible.

> The story of redemption in the Spirit made sense of the "ups and downs" of the daily life of the participants. In the Spirit they walked with the children of Israel, the prophets, the apostles and early church believers. In the Spirit they anticipated the great marriage supper of the Lamb at the last day. In the Spirit the blessing and trials of each day were interpreted as part of the one story of redemption. Thus, by interpreting their daily life and worship in terms of the significant events of biblical history, their own lives and actions were given significance. Everybody became a witness to Calvary and his or her own crucifixion with Christ, the biblical Pentecost and a personal Pentecost, the healings of the disciples and his or her own healing and so on.[2]

The Pentecostal preacher inhales from the biblical narrative, only to breathe it out again so it might be inhaled by the congregants, until they

1. Twain, *Mark Twain's Own Autobiography*, xliii.
2. Land, *Pentecostal Spirituality*, 73.

are all breathing the same air: the air of story. And when these narratives—from Scripture, from the congregation, from the preacher—are all mixed together in the same atmosphere, the result is testimony.

At the end of the day, the preacher is testifying. That is it. He is testifying like a witness in a courtroom. He is testifying like a witness to a jury of witnesses, only the jury cannot remain silent. "Well!" "Preach it, preacher!" "Uh-huh!" "Alright now!" Pentecostal preaching is just back-and-forth testimony, one witness to the others. "We cannot help speaking about what we have seen and heard," Peter and John protest in Acts 4:20.

This is the testimonial preaching you will hear in a traditional Pentecostal church. It fits the definition that James Baldwin gave to writing a novel: "To tell as much of the truth as one can bear, and then a little more."[3] Even if the preacher has notes, the sermon will for the most part be extemporaneous, because God knows you can't plan what you really might feel about the grit of life that day or at any other given moment. The message may also be chanted or sung, defying the Protestant Reformation's emphasis on the preached word, as if any word could be more significant than those words that come from the heart that are too guttural to be spoken apart from the solace of music or rhythm. And above all else, the sermon is not really a sermon, in the sense of a presentation people listen to. Instead, it is a dialogue that all participate in, with the requisite calling back and forth, the energy transferring from one side of the room to the other until no one and everyone is the preacher.

In her novel *NW*, Zadie Smith tells of a room full of high-society people who will not permit the entrance of the main character, Leah: "Everything behind those French doors is full and meaningful. The gestures, the glances, the conversation that can't be heard. How do you get to be so full? And so full of only meaningful things?"[4] The crescendos of a thousand Pentecostal sermons I heard as a child remind me of such a hidden room whose front door is quickly disappearing. Nowadays you'll have to go to either the country or the other side of the tracks to hear such preaching. It is questionable whether my children will ever hear any of it. These are real losses.

3. Baldwin, *Cross of Redemption*, 35.
4. Smith, *NW: A Novel*, 16.

You can chart this transition from preaching to presentation by tracking our nation's most popular televangelists, so you know the change can't be all good. Not long ago, a Pentecostal firebrand named Rod Parsley was the leading American preacher, sweating, hollering, and dancing himself into more households than any other. He wore brightly colored suits and lived in Ohio. His sermon titles were big and brash: "It's Jubilee!," "Your (Double) Breakthrough Is Now!," "It's a New Season!" He seemed angry most of the time, or excessively constipated. Never a dull moment.

Now Parsley is a has-been and the main event is Joel Osteen, who hails from the sunny, prosperous, never-ending suburb of Houston, Texas. Sporting whitened teeth and gelled hair, Osteen speaks with a pleasing drawl and never gets excited. He gives self-help talks peppered with a few Bible verses. He allows upbeat interviews to the morning news shows. His books are perky and platinum-selling and not built around strange Old Testament themes (*Your Best Life Now*). He is an experienced joke-teller. He does not get sweaty on camera. His sermons are as boring and lifeless as white bread.

Frankly, I can't stand Rod Parsley's preaching. Yet I miss him. At least he was interesting and never toned down his religion. What happened?

I guess we Pentecostal preachers got wise to the world. Like Adam and Eve, we realized our nakedness, realized that our preaching was socially unacceptable, so we started learning not so much how to preach but how to make businesslike presentations loosely based on passages of Scripture. We stopped gathering together to just dwell inside the text to see what might happen and instead began to explain it, to chart it, to study it in Greek, for heaven's sake. The preacher isn't reminding everyone of what they already know; he is now expected to teach people what they presumably don't yet know. In the process, the Bible has become a self-help book, the whole grand narrative trivialized so that it can be hopelessly "relevant" to our puny little lives. We turned symphonies into Power Point presentations. It is all classic cultural assimilation.

I wonder a lot about Jesus's preaching. Would his material play in the suburbs today? He was obviously a brilliant communicator. "The crowds were amazed at his teaching," we are told at the end of the Sermon on the Mount in Matthew 7. On the other side of the coin, it was not a promising sign that his first official sermon in Luke's telling almost got him thrown off the nearest cliff (4:29). But in between these extremes lay most of Jesus's sermons, which were given in parables. And like vivid Pentecostal preaching, parables lured people in.

Jesus would be a frustrating pastor because of all the parables he liked to spin. He did not often answer questions directly, even simple ones. "Who is my neighbor?" Jesus was asked in Luke 10:29. In reply, Jesus started on again: "A man was going down from Jerusalem . . ." If your preacher went about like this all the time, you would move to Houston to sit under Joel Osteen.

Other rabbis told parables around this time as well, but nobody could turn them out like Jesus. His stories are often hair-raising in their graphic detail. The poor man Lazarus with dogs licking his sores. The unnamed rich man who longs for a fingertip of water on his tongue. The wicked tenants who plot to kill the landholder's son. The scheming, shrewd manager who somehow wins "employee of the month" after stealing from the estate. You can almost feel the crowds leaning in when Jesus preaches his parables. In fact, the listeners are always involved, interrupting and questioning. There is no parable without emotion, without response. You can feel the *imagination* of the parabolic event, Jesus leading his listeners into Coleridge's definition of the same: "the willing suspension of disbelief." Jesus's sermons are not teachings so much as "language events," in the words of Eta Linnemann—events that require the listeners to make a decision.[5]

So Jesus's parables consisted of narrative, dialogue, testimony, improvisation, emotion, and response? That all sounds pretty Pentecostal to me. Maybe we were on the right track without ever realizing it.

Of the impulse that led him to write his most famous book, Henri Nouwen says,

> Speak to us about the deepest yearning of our hearts, about our many wishes, about hope; not about the many strategies for survival, but about trust; not about new methods of satisfying our emotional needs, but about love. Speak to us about a vision larger than our changing perspective and about a voice deeper than the clamorings of our mass media. Yes, speak to us about something or someone greater than ourselves. Speak to us about . . . God. . . . Speak from that place in your heart where you are most yourself.[6]

Yes and amen. May our preachers learn to speak again.

5. Cited in Jones, *Studying the Parables*, 6.
6. Nouwen, *Life of the Beloved*, 25.

7

Liturgy

_____

A high school stage play is more polished than this service we have been
rehearsing since the year one. In two thousand years, we have not worked out
the kinks. We positively glorify them. Week after week we witness the same
miracle: that God is so mighty he can stifle his own laughter. Week after week,
we witness the same miracle: that God, for reasons unfathomable, refrains
from blowing our dancing bear act to smithereens. Week after week Christ
washes the disciples' dirty feet, handles their very toes, and repeats, It is all
right—believe it or not—to be people. Who can believe it?

—ANNIE DILLARD

You wouldn't think that Pentecostals are by and large reflective folks.
People without social status are generally not reading literary reviews,
scouring Zagat's to find the top steakhouses, or subscribing to _Consumer
Reports_ for the best deals on things. I still don't know what goes on at a
five-star hotel, much less how a hotel earns these stars. Historically, we've
had just about nothing to do with film or the arts in general (outside of
bluegrass music), so most of us wouldn't know what passes for good there
either. But it's the oddest thing—we invented the concept of rating a worship service on a sliding scale. And the scale can be charted by the extent to
which we demolish any hint of liturgy.

In many streams of Christian tradition, *liturgy* is the everyday term used to represent the elements of the Sunday morning worship service: the hymns, the readings, the sermon, the prayers. *Liturgy* is an ancient word, stretching back to the sacred priestly services of the classical Greek age: the *leiturgos*. In Pentecostal circles, *liturgy* is not a word we use. It is something of a dirty word. It is "what the Catholics do"—the droll ritualism of the weekly Mass. In 1947, Pope Pius XII presented the most pace-setting encyclical on the current liturgy for Catholics:

> You are surely well aware that this Apostolic See has always made careful provision for the schooling of the people committed to its charge in the correct spirit and practice of the liturgy; and that it has been no less careful to insist that the sacred rites should be performed with due external dignity.[1]

It sounds like the pope is saying that true liturgy is defined by "external dignity." Pentecostals are more likely to appropriate the words of David in 1 Samuel 6:21–22 to describe our worship: "I will celebrate before the LORD. I will become even more undignified than this, and I will be humiliated in my own eyes." Indignity, rather than the pope's sophisticated tractate, is often the Pentecostal brand of worship.

Language is peculiar in that it can still function somewhat effectively without conveying much specific meaning at all. If you don't believe that, just watch the cable news channels. As a boy and then a teenager, I'm certain that I could not have defined the term *liturgy* if my life had been on the line, but I can easily recall the mental images that were associated with the word. Maybe our memories are just better at hanging on to the pictures, or maybe the pictures are the greater reality before they get manipulated down to controllable words—words that can be sized up beside other more or less powerful words.

When I was a kid, *liturgy* conveyed a specific vision of church. I imagined a small, stone-walled cathedral—the weighty gray stones that are cemented together in a hodgepodge and left bare and jagged, the kind you hardly see at all anymore except in castles. I can see them in my mind still. I thought of stained glass windows on the walls of this cathedral, of course, but not imposing or grand enough to overpower the coldness, the grayness, of the stones creeping every which way on top of one another all the way

1. *Mediator Dei*, 6, cited in Ege, *Finding My Way to Salvation*, 96.

to the ceiling, the cracks between them like spider webs wrapping up the stones. In my recollection of this childhood memory of the stone cathedral, there were hardly any worshippers in the place, and they were faceless (or was it that they never turned around to let me see their faces?). A panoramic view isn't left with me, if I ever had it, nor anything outside, just a slanted view upward from the bottom of the back wall toward the front of the church—not centered enough to see the altar or the robed pastor, but I knew he was there, in a black robe with hair that matched the walls, all the time chanting lost words in some language as musty as the smell of those stones. Nothing ever changed in that church, which is perhaps why I can still remember such an early vision of this mental association that accompanied the term *liturgy*.

Later, in high school, I came to believe that liturgy was what the rich people did at church, which made sense to my teenage mind because successful people like to get things done, and liturgy makes no bones about when the thing will get done. You may show up to the cathedral on a Sunday morning a little nervous about what could happen, until somebody passes you a sheet with the liturgy listed right there in black and white: Opening Hymn, Prayer, Reading, Sermon, Benediction. Now you can relax and monitor the situation. If you don't much care for the reading from Lamentations that day, you can slip out for a quick smoke without missing a beat, then just pick up wherever it suits you. I had heard that people at the liturgy churches smoked cigarettes on Sunday mornings.

I had a high school history teacher whose wife made them wealthy by selling something expensive, and he bragged to the class once that their Methodist services lasted fifty-five minutes on the dot. He may as well have told me that he snorted cocaine each morning before preparing his lectures. I was appalled. Had I known then what I know now—that Methodist pastors preach according to a prescribed set of annual texts called the lectionary—I probably would have staged a walkout. How on earth could worship be confined to a timed liturgical script?

Because we mainstream Pentecostals were anti-liturgy, we assumed that we held the corner on the market when it came to savoring a good worship service. After all, the liturgy churches had to be more or less the same week to week. On what grounds did they determine the quality of a service? In the liturgy churches, even the sermons—*the sermons*, for heaven's sake— were scripted and read straight from the page. I wondered why they didn't just mail out the liturgy with the sermon and a cassette of the hymns to save everyone the trouble of showing up.

Only the really uppity Pentecostal churches had very general "Order of Service" sheets, and when these caught on with the rest of our movement it was sort of understood that they were printed up to be ignored, so that we could subsequently brag about ignoring them. When I was in junior high school, however, we attended one of those upper-echelon churches in a big city, and I remember my shock at a Wednesday night Bible study when the ushers passed outlines of the night's teaching down each of the pews. It felt to me like they were distributing scorpions. I had no idea we allowed that kind of thing. If we kept following this course, I reasoned, we'd soon be smoking Winstons in the pews, chanting in Latin.

After we had moved from the uppity, outline-handout church back to a normal Pentecostal congregation in a shady part of town where your car was likely to be broken into, determining whether or not we had really "had church," as we put it, was finally easy again, as easy as back in Snellville. If one of three factors was in play, good church was had by all. The first factor was Elizabeth.

Elizabeth was an old lady in our little choir who was at that stage in life most everybody gets to of always looking kind of detached and dumbstruck, a diminutive little thing trying her best, I suppose, to just get up and make a go at it every day. I don't ever recall her speaking, singing a solo, clapping or lifting her hands. For all I knew she didn't actually sing in the choir, just stood up there waiting for her moment to validate the whole experience. We knew that we had finally got to having church when that old woman screamed.

I still shudder to think about it, that scream. It was like something out of Alfred Hitchcock, only lengthier, dragging out inhumanly longer than anyone could imagine her little lungs could handle. We'd be joined together in an act of prayer or worship, our eyes closed, hands lifted toward heaven, and she'd let loose something you felt in your bones before it reverberated outward to your very scalp, like she was screaming from inside of you. If you hadn't relieved yourself before the service, things could really get ugly. For the rest of us, it was the signal that church had been had and we could now go home.

But Elizabeth was old and frail and certainly couldn't be counted on to let loose each week, since every scream probably took at least a few months off her diminishing life span (such was the energy, the potency of it), so we had two more liturgy-busting criteria. Oddly enough, the first was skipping what for Pentecostals continues to be the most esteemed part of the service—the preaching.

"We didn't even get to the preachin' today!" is a common refrain heard after a highly rated Pentecostal worship service, meaning that the music just sort of raised itself and everything else into a crescendo of prayer or celebration down at the altar. You can feel it coming along the way, an emotional freight train bringing the whole experience to a tipping point. The preacher scraps his notes, the musicians stay on call, and our kind of church happens.

The third and final gauge for determining the quality of a Pentecostal worship service has less to do with quality than quantity. This one really gets the symbolic goat of the liturgists, which feels good to do. Say what you want about us, we're consistent folks, and to us a greater volume of something—pretty much anything—equals a more satisfying experience. This is why we love to eat at buffet restaurants. If there are too many of us for a table out, we stay in and potluck on the church grounds. To us, the more the merrier, and that formula certainly applies to the length of our services.

You would think that cutting out the preaching would shorten the service, but this is not so. The worship and prayer and hoopla that take its place always last much longer. If it doesn't, then there was no reason to skip the preaching to begin with. See, even though most of us haven't met a liturgy-church member, much less been to a service like that—and Lord knows they wouldn't be caught dead in our church—there's something satisfying about feeling like you are ticking them off. I didn't say a word to my history teacher who bragged about their hourlong gathering, but the next week when our music took an hour by itself, I felt somehow vindicated.

Remember that we're talking about liturgy here, and the Pentecostal commitment to not having one. Add to this our aforementioned belief in unmediated authority, which means that no one has the right to tell you that you shouldn't be singing or preaching, no matter how God-awful you sound, and it becomes pretty clear that quality control is not our bag. So if you can't go for quality in the service, go for quantity. Do whatever it is that you do longer than anyone else, and the job has been done. Since so many of our members punch a clock at work, it has always made a lot of sense to see things this way.

❧

You are probably catching on to the quandary presented by the Pentecostal disdain for liturgy. The fact that I can describe these predictable patterns of our worship services says it all. If not having a liturgy is our liturgy, it ends up looking a lot like liturgy: a louder, bigger, and longer liturgy, but a liturgy just the same. But there is a subtle difference. Liturgy is a script, and who would think to read the script of a play while the play is being performed right in front of you? Who doesn't revisit the same favorite films and books over and over, all the while knowing exactly what will happen? Perhaps the rise of American impromptu theater in the last few years can be seen as a response to the scriptedness of the predictable schlock that Hollywood churns out. But Pentecostals invented such improvisation.

We knew what would happen no less than the Catholics knew when to kneel, the Methodists when to chant back "and also with You." We knew when to listen for Elizabeth's scream, but it scared us half to death every time. We knew exactly where the preacher was going, which was probably where he went last week and the week before, but we goaded him on like he was an oracle. And we knew when we just couldn't leave the altar, and maybe it was there that we actually did, if only for a moment, break out of the man-made liturgy, that corruptive need for control that is slowly destroying us all.

"Worship is an act of poetic imagination that aims to reconstrue the world," Walter Brueggemann contends. "It is an act of imagination, by which I mean it presents lived reality in images, figures and metaphors that defy our conventional structures of plausibility and that host alternative scenarios of reality that cut beyond our conventional perceptual field."[2]

Maybe it is this "act of imagination" that birthed Pentecostalism in the first place. Maybe it is such "alternative scenarios" that we are all of us longing for with an inexpressible longing, because if we expressed it we'd find a way to cure it with a script of our own devising. "There must be another script," our souls believe, one not written by the hands of men, as Jeremiah prophesied, but a script of flesh and blood etched into our very hearts. "I will put my law in their minds and write it on their hearts. I will be their God and they will be my people."

At its best and at its worst, this is Pentecostal liturgy: a no-frills encounter with the holy that, even though we are all there expecting it, somehow happens in a way we can't quite expect.

And the crazy thing is that next week, it will happen all over again.

2. Brueggemann, *Mandate to Difference*, 117.

8

Revival

For no sooner had he begun (in the application of his sermon) to invite all
sinners to believe in Christ, than four persons sunk down close to him, almost
in the same moment. One of them lay without either sense or motion; a
second trembled exceeding; the third had strong convulsions all over his body,
but made no noise, unless by groans; the fourth, equally convulsed, called
upon God, with strong cries and tears. From this time, I trust, we shall all
suffer God to carry on His own work in the way that pleaseth Him.

—JOHN WESLEY, REFLECTING ON GEORGE WHITFIELD'S
REVIVAL MEETING

Spiritual revivals have a special place in the history of America. The early
history of the U.S. was shaped by a series of Great Awakenings, led by
trailblazing evangelists who would stop at nothing to command the communities of our land to repent before God. There was Jonathan Edwards
of the eighteenth century, known for his hair-raising sermons, seasoned
with fire and brimstone (the most famous one titled "Sinners in the Hands
of an Angry God"). George Whitfield was letting loose at the same time as
Edwards. His voice could be heard a mile away, so he preached to ten thousand at a time. Even the skeptical Benjamin Franklin was known to slip into
the crowd, always unbelieving yet impressed by Whitfield's oratory.

The nineteenth century in America was also shaped by powerful revivalist preachers. Charles Finney preached to thousands with no notes and seemingly no preparation, building the Underground Railroad and writing his masterwork, *Revivals of Religion*. D. L. Moody, a self-avowed layman, led revivalism into the twentieth century, tirelessly preaching to some ten million people in his lifetime and establishing Moody Bible Institute and the Y.M.C.A. In our time, the evangelist Billy Graham has preached the Christian message to more people than anyone in history.

Individual improvement is so central to the American experience and ethos, making America the perfect seedbed for Christian revivalism. Revivals in the seventeenth and eighteenth centuries were like moralistic groupthink, a Woodstock of religious proportions. "Come, let us return to the LORD," the prophet Hosea told Israel. "After two days he will revive us; on the third day he will restore us, that we may live in his presence" (6:1–2). Incidentally, this promise of revival is the closest reference in the Old Testament to the resurrection of Christ in the New.

Although such societal, epic revivals have faded into the textbooks of history, the spirit of revivalism is still alive and well in Christian congregations all across America and around the globe. Protestants of many stripes now mark periods of revival on our calendars, save the dates come what may, and hold them every year, like a holiday.

The first step in understanding the nature of a "Pentecostal revival" is to not get it mixed up with the Baptist kind. It was the Baptists who made the concept of local church revivals famous. For them, revivals are hosted a few times a year and entail setting aside a week or so to have worship services each night with a guest evangelist. These Baptist revival services aren't really any different from what they do every week on Sunday morning, except for the visiting minister filling the pulpit. Billy Graham got his start doing this kind of thing on a larger scale, and his original evangelistic crusades were called revivals. Let me reiterate: this is *not* what Pentecostals mean when they talk about revival.

Sure, we had plenty of weeklong church-a-thons when I was growing up, but you sure as sugar couldn't confuse them with business as usual. The entire reason they were held was to annihilate such routine. We had routines for the sole purpose of busting out of other routines.

Like the Baptists, itinerant evangelists led our Pentecostal revivals. Like the revivalists of old, they traveled anywhere an audience could be found. But our evangelists were nothing like the Baptist ones. Billy Graham would have bored my church to tears.

I heard dozens of evangelists growing up in various revival services, but three come to mind most prominently. I witnessed all three of these evangelists during my teenage years. One was a British ex-soccer player—perhaps the only Pentecostal evangelist I ever heard who came off as debonair. On the surface, the guy looked, acted, and dressed normal, even cultured. He spoke with a pleasant, engaging voice, and in Georgia most anybody with a foreign accent sounded smart back then, even people from New Jersey. What's more, like a rock star the guy actually had roadies—a small following that boosted our normal attendance when he came through town. Honestly, I can't remember a thing the guy said except an offhand remark about the effects of Coca-Cola on one's tooth enamel, presumably in the context of St. Paul's admonition that "your body is a temple of the Holy Spirit" (1 Cor 6:19). Anyhow, nobody was there because of the Englishman's speaking ability. That would have made it a Baptist revival. It didn't matter one way or the other whether the guy could preach himself through John 3:16. We were really there for the falling over.

This will sound awfully strange to outsiders, but in the last few decades falling on the floor has been a hallmark of Pentecostal revivalism. And it can happen anytime. Although most pastors reserved it for the climactic time of prayer at the altar at the end of the service, the British guy would walk up to some nobody in the back of the sanctuary while in the middle of a sermon sub-point about tooth enamel and cause him to fall backward onto the ground. He was perfectly nice about it and didn't do anything to egg it on. He'd just ask you to stand, then take your hand and whisper "Jesus," and you'd fall over. The sermon was just liturgy, really—just an excuse to walk around the room with a microphone so that anybody who wanted to could fall down.

Eventually, the falling became routine, since we figured out that it was the point of things, so we assigned the larger men of the congregation to operate as catchers to help the fallers. After all, nothing will end an ecstatic experience of the Spirit quicker than slamming the back of your head on a wooden pew, so the catchers followed the British guy around the sanctuary to make sure the fallers enjoyed a safe landing.

Another problem altogether was posed by the female fallers. In the Southern Pentecostal tradition, it was once considered sinful for women to wear pants, but they sure would have come in handy during revivals. If you think bashing your head against a pew will quench the Spirit, try getting flashed by an old Pentecostal lady. Our solution, then, was to assign, in addition to the big male catchers, a few women to follow the British guy around with blankets to quickly throw over the ladies' legs after the catchers had done their job. I doubt St. Paul ever preached with an entourage like that, and it made for quite a spectacle, all those catchers and cloth-bearers hovering around the speaker as he weaved through the room. When most everybody was laid out on the floor, we got up and went home. Revival had been had.

Every other evangelist I can recall was from the South, of course, and therefore lacked the more sophisticated approach of the British guy. Southerners generally just go about getting after whatever is to be gotten, so when the falling movement came over from Britain or wherever, our Southern evangelists put the thing on steroids. No more of this quiet praying, hand in hand, with individuals—that was tedious, boring. We needed a system to get people falling quicker and in greater numbers, and a second evangelist who held several revivals at my church had found just the way.

First, instead of taking people gently by the hand and whispering the name of Jesus, this evangelist actually hurled his Bible through the air at people, which proved a quicker method of making them fall. If a hurtled Bible hit you in the gut, you fell down. And as if that weren't hard enough to believe, I'm telling you that the guy had major-league accuracy. I wondered if he had a pregame warm-up in some kind of makeshift bullpen in the parking lot, a stack of Bibles beside the pitcher's mound. He could hit you square in the sternum from thirty or forty feet away. It was amazing, the Roger Clemens of book throwing.

Second, once the service really got hopping, this evangelist would get really efficient and start making people fall in large groups. He spoke at some pretty big meetings sometimes, so I guess this method made more sense in the long run than the Bible throwing. Plus, he was an older guy, and if most big leaguers can only throw seventy or eighty fastballs during a game, he certainly had his limits too. So when things reached their climax, he'd just line people up, wave his hand, and they'd fall over like dominoes. It was like a spiritual assembly line. Of course, the catchers and cloth-bearers couldn't keep up with this kind of efficiency, and this evangelist didn't seem to give a flip. He was from the South, and if you fell backward under the power of the Spirit and split your head open on a sharp object, or even on another faller's head, then it wasn't the Spirit to begin with, just you playing along. And a guy that goes around pitching Bibles at people simply isn't into playing along; he *wants* you to get hurt if you're faking it. He's not icing his arm for an hour after every service for nothing.

The third evangelist came when I was a few years older, and he wasn't quite as experienced or colorful as the other guys. He wore brightly colored suits with knee-length jackets, like a circus ringmaster, which is one of the many contributions of Christian television to the Pentecostal scene, along with weird hair. I'm sure he co-opted this style from the black preachers on TV, and it's sad that nobody told him he couldn't pull it off. He couldn't really pull off preaching either, but he compensated for this with a lot of shouting, running back and forth, and provocative brainteasers. The guy actually said that earthquakes were caused by hell enlarging itself with greater numbers of the damned. I never paid much attention in geology class, so this was some startling information. Why hadn't my Christian school teacher covered this in the earth science material?

Neil Diamond captured our theatrical revivalism all too well in his now classic hit song "Brother Love's Travelling Salvation Show," the sawdust trail of Pentecostal evangelists making a living off their own mystique. But when I was in college, everything changed. The concept of revival was transformed from falling down in a weeklong series of services a few times a year to going for revival all the time. It became a buzzword in the Pentecostal tradition like no other, as if you could just say the word and people would fall down. Prayer meetings became focused on getting this thing called revival to happen and to stick around as long as possible.

I think this shift from revival as a planned moment to an ongoing reality comes from our search for identity. Pentecostals had been looking for a buzzword to call our very own for a long time. Baptists had "saved" and mainline Protestants had "social justice." Mennonites and Quakers had "pacifism." But we didn't have anything all our own. We couldn't rightly claim the Holy Spirit, since everybody else did too, so when "revival" became the rage, we built a bandwagon and rode it until it broke. It all started in a town called Brownsville.

God is odd, and if you don't believe that then you can't begin to understand a thing about Pentecostal spirituality. In 1995, a church called the Brownsville Assembly of God in Florida was having a normal set of revival services that they decided to extend for a week, then another, then another and another. After a few months, they announced that it looked like "revival" had landed for good and that as a result they would have services every night for as long as it lasted. It lasted years, and people flocked to the spectacle from around the world. In its second year, I was one of the flock.

When I attended the Brownsville revival, I honestly didn't see the big deal. People waited in line all day to get in the place, but it wasn't much different than the revival services I had always known. The music was long and traditional, a lot of Southern foot-stomping stuff about kicking the devil around and calling God up on the telephone and such, and the preaching was a throwback to the holiness preachers of old, where anything remotely fun was sinful and if Jesus wasn't your very first thought when you woke up then you were surely backslidden and needed to repent in order to avoid the divine wrath that is to come. At the end of every service they sang a song about running to the sacrificial altar of God in the Old Testament temple, and people sprinted from all corners of the sanctuary up to the front, where the evangelist knocked them over. The only original element I could find in the whole experience was that people physically shook under the influence of the Spirit. Some of them walked in the building shaking like an epileptic before the service even got started; others shook when the evangelist prayed for them. I guess it makes sense. Falling down is a rather fleeting experience, but you can pretty much go about your normal business while shaking, which stretches out that time under the Spirit a good bit longer and also allows you to function.

This pattern of ongoing revival spread throughout Pentecostal churches everywhere. A campus group began to pray fervently that a similar "revival" would hit our Christian college. Folks at Brownsville wrote books and had conferences about how to get such a thing going. In turn, churches started meeting every night for weeks and months and proclaiming that revival had arrived. It was as if at any moment it could strike like a tornado and turn things upside down. Incredible testimonies of healing, salvation, and miracles ensued. It seemed a bit sensationalist to me then, or even like a convenient cop-out, an alternative to actually going about the rather ordinary life of faith, but now I'm not so sure.

❧

Something Pentecostals seem to have understood before everyone else is that the gospel is *apocalyptic*. That means that the gospel is cosmic in scope, concerned with bringing human history and God's work with creation to its ultimate fulfillment where evil will be eradicated and "God will be all in all," as Saint Paul says in 1 Corinthians 15. According to New Testament scholar N. T. Wright,

> Biblical apocalyptic is all about God's future breaking in to the present, seen in glimpses, known above all in Jesus, and best expressed not in abstract theology or even in preaching, but, yes, in genuine and visionary art. Apocalyptic, both in form and in biblical content, is not about the denial of the present creation, but about the overcoming of its sorrows and the realizing of its promise. Apocalyptic is the key to understanding, and re-expressing, the beauty of God.[1]

I wonder if anyone at all could remain standing under the actual realization of such apocalyptic truth. There is a great sense in which those campy revival services even sought to compel God's future into the present by way of inviting the literal glory, the weightiness of God, into the room. Say what you want about it, we at least took the scope of the gospel seriously, a scope that much of the rest of the body of Christ continues to ignore.

I live in a neighborhood that is so dreadfully suburban that Radiohead's famous song "Fake Plastic Trees" could have been written about it. Every lawn is perfectly manicured, and people actually replace their regular driveways with these fancy cobblestone ones, as if they are somehow better than cement. Everyone tips 20 percent. Every house has at least two SUVs, preferably with V8 engines. Everybody waits until they're forty to start having kids. Everybody votes Republican. And everybody is a Christian. I tried a few nearby churches when we first moved here, but they were like Christian versions of *Oprah*, which must take some serious effort to pull off, since Oprah is better than everyone at everything she does. I made the mistake of visiting an evangelical "Bible church" on Easter Sunday and

---

1. Wright, "Apocalyptic and the Beauty of God," para. 7.

have never felt more depressed in my life—the resurrection of mankind packaged into some nonsense about how "God will give you strength to overcome obstacles." I've seen richer theology in comic books.

In neighborhoods like this, Catholics, mainline Protestants, and evangelicals alike have tended to boil down the apocalyptic elements of the gospel into pleasant edicts of moral behavior, a downsizing of the grand narrative of God's work in the world to personal ethics, resulting in the kind of Christian who is syrupy nice to people and never late on the mortgage payment. Hans Conzelmann, a Lutheran who wrote one of the most famous studies of the books of Luke and Acts, actually stated, "Luke does not describe the Christian life in spiritual but in ethical categories."[2] Well, okay, Hans, but you've kind of got the cart before the unicorn, don't you think?

Sure, the New Testament is laced with ethical teaching, but most of it is not much more than various restatements of Old Testament teachings. What is truly new, however, is the way in which people hear them. Jesus would certainly be a bit easier to stomach if he just showed up in the synagogue for a teaching session, and perhaps people would have listened to what he had to say all the same. But when he unfurls a withered hand or morphs a couple of fish into lunch on the grounds, aren't his moral messages heard differently? It's clear that Jesus wasn't just a nice guy in the helping business; his miracles, and thus his teaching, meant something fantastical about God's nuclear inbreaking into the world that changed everything for everybody and called for an equally nuclear response.

Get into the ministry of Jesus's disciples in the book of Acts, and it's the same drill. Something unreasonably supernatural happens, and some apostle announces that God did it, so everybody who saw it better get themselves together in time for the apocalyptic end of all things. Not much happens that God doesn't initiate by way of something that's just plain crazy: babbling tongues, people falling out of windows to their deaths, angels walking around like men, blinding epiphanies. Like it or not, Acts isn't some religious version of William Bennett's *Book of Virtues* (ironically, or perhaps appropriately, Bennett compulsively gambled away all the royalties thereof). It's the apocalyptic announcement that the world has suddenly been made different, not by way of some new moral teaching but because God decided to rectify the cosmic situation on his own. And when God steps on the scene, things get uncontainable in a hurry.

2. Conzelmann, *Theology of St. Luke*, 105.

One of my favorite examples of the hilarity of this new world is in Acts 16, where Paul and Silas perform an exorcism that results in their getting beat up and thrown into prison. In response, they do what genuine losers always do: they sing their hearts out to the amusement of everybody else, playing that Pentecostal role as idiots of the underclass. They sing like there is a monkey on their shoulder and a crank in their hand, bloodied as they are. Apparently they hit some particular hymn just the way God likes it, and an earthquake levels the place until the gates shoot open and the prisoners are all strewn everywhere, trying to figure out how and why they are free. And wouldn't you know it, a whole pagan household comes to faith. "Sirs, what must I do to be saved?" the hardened warden asks (16:30). No impressive liturgy, no memorable preaching, no self-help steps, just a bunch of singing and shaking and falling to the ground, and the incomprehensible joy of a crusty jailer's dead heart being finally and completely revived. "The jailer brought them into his house and set a meal before them; he was filled with joy because he had come to believe in God—he and his whole family" (16:34).

Sounds to me like a dose of that kind of revival would do all of us some good.

9

Tongues

---

*Now, do not go from this meeting and talk about tongues, but try to get
people saved!*

—WILLIAM SEYMOUR

It is safe to say that the average man on the street, if he has heard of a
Pentecostal, associates us with one of our odder habits: what is typically called "speaking in tongues." We take this phrase from the King James
translation of the book of Acts in the New Testament, a translation that was
hammered out in Shakespearean times. You might also call the habit, more
contemporarily, "speaking in languages."

Speaking in tongues is what Pentecostals became known for early on,
especially during the Azusa Street Revival. Its leader, William Seymour,
tried his best to focus people's attention not on the phenomenon of tongues
but on the lifestyle that such Spirit-empowerment produced. "If you get
angry, or speak evil or backbite, I care not how many tongues you may have,
you have not the baptism with the Holy Spirit," he preached.[1] Well put. Still,
it is hard not to focus on a group of people who spontaneously burst into
shouting a bunch of syllables that sound like gibberish.

---

1. Cited in Friesen, *Norming the Abnormal*, 58.

"We believe in speaking with other tongues as the Spirit gives utterance," my denomination's faith statement reads, "and that it is the initial evidence of the baptism in the Holy Ghost." As if speaking in tongues were not aberrant enough, this statement seriously upped the ante. If you don't speak in tongues, you haven't really had a full experience of the Holy Spirit, we declared. The gift of tongues is the entrance requirement into Spirit baptism and the complete Christian life. If you don't do it, according to our particular tradition, you're not a bona fide Pentecostal.

Our motives in this effort to encourage the gift of tongues have always been pure, but slapping a bunch of strictures on the activity of the Holy Spirit is tricky business at best, like trying to tame the wind. At worst, we can dress up to play the part of God. Certainly, God "does not change like the shifting shadows," James 1:17 says, but neither is God beholden to formulas. In erring to the formulaic side, I have seen and heard all kinds of personal stories about well-meaning Pentecostals trying to "help" others receive the gift of tongues, and the stories range from the horrific to the hokey.

Growing up, there were plenty of altar calls to receive the Holy Spirit by way of the "sign" of speaking in tongues (signage is the language for the gift used in Mark 16:17). People often testified of "seeking" the gift for many months. (One new convert who was in seeking mode remarked, "The Holy Ghost sure is an elusive thing, ain't He?") Seekers would crowd the altar, and holy huddles would form around them, swaying back and forth, everyone praying out loud, eight, ten, twelve hands on the seeker's shoulders and head. At some point after the seeker had been thoroughly leaned on by the group, someone would take the lead. The leader would stand face to face with the seeker, and the oral exam would begin. "Speak out! Speak anything that comes to mind!" I have seen people pat the chin of the speaker with the back of their hand up and down, over and over. Judge us if you must, but the Catholics believe that the communion wine transubstantiates into real blood. Are we not also allowed some hocus-pocus?

If there were Holy Ghost blockages that the prayer huddles could not break through, individual attention was warranted. The pros were called in with tactical stents. One friend of mine was taken to a room and given practice words. "You can do it!" the pro said to bolster him. In my mind the scene looks like an interrogation room in an episode of *Law and Order*, a hanging light bulb over a metal desk, the pro with a walkie-talkie strapped to his belt to relay any breakthrough. Even with such serious help, my friend never did speak in tongues.

In fact, I know all kinds of people who identify with Pentecostalism but who never crossed the tongues threshold. My denomination is still trying to figure out what to do with them. Jesus told Nicodemus in John 3:8 that "the Spirit blows wherever it pleases." "The Holy Ghost sure is an elusive thing, ain't he?"

I remember the time it all first hit me. It was at a Pentecostal summer camp fashioned to launch such experiences, and I was fourteen. I had been praying for the gift of tongues. It occurred without the conventional fanfare. I knelt down at a dented metal chair in a room with paneled walls and frayed carpet, and I just let loose. What did it feel like? Not like ecstasy or proclamation. I did not want to run the aisles, swing from the rafters, or tell anyone about it. I wanted to fall asleep, enmeshed, enshrouded in what felt like perfect love. Whatever on earth or in heaven I was or wasn't saying, it felt like God understood and was pleased.

There are all kinds of smart studies on the phenomenon of speaking in tongues, typically called glossalalia in academic circles (from the Greek words *glossa*, "language," and *laleo*, "to speak"). The experience of tongues is not particular to Pentecostals, or even to Christians, but there does seem to be a common thread uniting those who participate: *glossalalia* is the language of the underclass. In the words of Randall Balmer, a professor of religion at Barnard University, "It provides a voice to people who feel they have no voice."[2]

I fear that such a definition might be interpreted as Marxist escapism—tongues as the opiate of the poor. I have never thought about tongues as some Christian version of *The Exorcist*, eyes rolling back into the head for a few moments of ecstasy, like a drug hit. Tongues are not the result of some kind of divine possession, which seems to be Paul's point in 1 Corinthians 14:32: "The spirits of prophets are subject to the control of prophets." Instead, at the most elemental level, tongues are about . . . tongues. Tongues

2. Miller, "BeliefWatch: Spirit Filled," par. 4.

are about language, about words. They beg the question, "Where does language come from and what does it mean to do?"

Even the most secular among us would readily acknowledge that the project of human language is in deep disrepair. The Quaker spiritualist Richard Foster contends,

> The tongue is our most powerful weapon of manipulation. A frantic stream of words flows from us because we are in a constant process of adjusting our public image. We fear so deeply what we think other people see in us that we talk in order to straighten out their understanding.[3]

Is not such evidence of the seductive and devalued power of language all around us? Just listen to the drone of the cable news wars, in which language is weaponized to the point where logic and objectivity become ninja stars to be thrown. And hasn't the larger church lost the battle of fighting devalued words with more devalued words that are theological in nature? "Christian language needs to be redeemed," Marcus Borg argues.[4] The church has not been able to save us from the word vomit we now swim in. We are all growing increasingly illiterate, shouting words back and forth that have little meaning and less value. All that matters is how sharply we can carve out the edges of our words.

Historically, Christian thought has been at the forefront of deconstructing the power of words to their constituent elements. There is plenty in the Bible about the potency of language (in our home, my mother was fond of quoting James 1:19, "Be quick to listen and slow to speak"), and this tradition has grown throughout the centuries. From the time of the first monk, Anthony the Great, in the third century, Christian monks have attacked word vomit with the powerful weapon of silence. Thomas Merton, the famous Trappist monk of the last century, renowned for his vows of silence, considered words to be the building blocks of the "false self" that we project onto others for our own perceived good.[5] His corrective: create silence. Søren Kierkegaard, a Danish theologian, wrote well over a century ago, "If I were a doctor and could prescribe just one remedy for all the ills of the modern world, I would prescribe silence."[6] Scores of similarly beautiful

---

3. Foster, *Celebration of Discipline*, 101.

4. Borg, *Speaking Christian*, 2.

5. Herron, *No Abiding Place*, 55.

6. Kanungo and Mendonca, *Ethical Dimensions of Leadership*, 101.

quotations on the power of silence from a thousand Christian mystics fill the pages of Christian literature.

Pentecostals are a part of this Christian trajectory but have attacked the same problem of word vomit from a dramatically different angle. You might say that the monastic tradition fought word inflation by raising the interest rates on language. The fewer words in play, the better their value. We Pentecostals did not follow this approach. As an underclass people, perhaps we saw silence as (in the words of Wendell Berry) "the distinguishing characteristic of absolute despair."[7] So we just decided to receive a whole new language altogether and, by doing so, to transcend despair.

In the New Testament, speaking in tongues began on a Jewish holiday called Pentecost (hence our name, Pentecostal), ten days or so after Jesus's ascension to heaven. The story is told in Acts 2 and represents the fulfillment of Jesus's last promise to the disciples in Acts 1:4–5: "Do not leave Jerusalem, but wait for the gift my Father promised, which you have heard me speak about. For John baptized with water, but in a few days you will be baptized with the Holy Spirit." And then, like a sandstorm, it hit. "All of them were filled with the Holy Spirit and began to speak in other tongues as the Spirit enabled them" (2:4). But that is only where the true story begins. It is the response of the onlookers to the phenomenon of speaking in tongues that constitutes the real meat of the narrative of Acts 2.

> Now there were staying in Jerusalem God-fearing Jews from every nation under heaven. When they heard this sound, a crowd came together in bewilderment, because each one heard their own language being spoken. Utterly amazed, they asked: "Aren't all these who are speaking Galileans? Then how is it that each of us hears them in our native language? Parthians, Medes and Elamites; residents of Mesopotamia, Judea and Cappadocia, Pontus and Asia, Phrygia and Pamphylia, Egypt and the parts of Libya near Cyrene; visitors from Rome (both Jews and converts to Judaism); Cretans and Arabs—we hear them declaring the wonders of God in our own tongues!" Amazed and perplexed, they asked one another, "What does this mean?" (2:5–12)

Languages old and new, spewing forth from the poor white trash of Galilee, now suddenly linguists. Indeed, what does such an event mean?

---

7. Berry, *What Are People For?*, 59.

It is hard to doubt that a very specific Old Testament text stands behind Acts 2, backlighting its meaning. It was way back in Genesis 11 where the nations highlighted in Acts 2 first endured their birth. There, the story of the Tower of Babel adds two great brush strokes to the burgeoning picture of Yahweh in the early days of humanity, a God who is ferociously particular. Those two new particularities painted in Genesis 11 are simply that (1) God doesn't care much for urban living, and (2) God really disdains dictatorial regimes, with their forced homogeneity. "Come, let us build ourselves a city, with a tower that reaches to the heavens, so that we may make a name for ourselves," the whiz kids of the Mesopotamian Valley devised, armed with their Apple computers, their new brickmaking technology and cool, horn-rimmed eyeglasses.

But God is not enthused.

"Come, let us go down and confuse their language so they will not understand each other," God decides after convening a council of Himself. "That is why it was called Babel—because there the LORD confused the language of the whole world," scattering them "across the face of the whole earth." In the Old Testament tradition, it is God's response to Babel that begets languages other than Hebrew. The project of multiple languages/tongues was meant to prevent human oppression at the Tower of Babel.

Of course, humanity found a way to derail that project of multiple languages as well. The Egyptian Empire would soon rise, forcing everything it could force on those who did not speak its language. Other empires came and went: the Babylonians gave way to the Persians, who gave way to Alexander the Great, who gave way to the Romans. One Tower of Babel was replaced with thousands more ethnically specific. By the time of Acts 2, there are too many towers to count—thousands of ethnic groups, all attempting to build bigger towers, to control the "foreigners" around them. And then the Holy Ghost descends, and in one fell swoop there are no more foreigners. A bunch of tongue-talking, illiterate Galileans turned all the towers to rubble.

At the day of Pentecost, the crisis whereby human languages separated the peoples of the earth, keeping them at odds with one another, is suddenly resolved. Oppression gives way to the birth pangs of unity. "We hear *them* declaring the wonders of God in our own tongues!" the astonished nations of the world proclaim. Languages that were once unintelligible are rendered intelligible. Confusion gives way to understanding. "What does this mean?"

Every Christian tradition has to answer this question for itself, of course. There were some in the Jerusalem crowd who simply assumed the disciples had been binging on Bloody Marys and mimosas, what with all their round-the-clock celebration of Jesus's supposed resurrection. We tongue-talkers are still considered imbalanced, if not loony.

But for Pentecostals, the answer to the question posed by the crowd still rings out. "What does this mean?" It means in part that God has visited us to change lives and to change history, to forge new creation from the old. This new creation, wrought by the Holy Spirit, requires not silence but declaration. This new creation requires wonder and bewilderment. Most of all, this new creation requires new tongues—the only intelligible language in God's new world. Ralph Waldo Emerson said that language is the archives of history.[8] God's new history operates on new words. Tongues are God's grand finale of holiness—the final sanctification of language itself so that all things might be made new.

T. S. Eliot wrote about his frustration in "trying to learn to use words, and every attempt is a wholly new start, and a different kind of failure."[9] If part of the meaning of the Tower of Babel is that no particular group of people has the corner on the word market, I am certainly not insinuating that Pentecostals have a corner on the tongues market. To make such a claim would be to transform tongues into propaganda. I am sure there are abuses and forgeries. As an adult, tongues make me uncomfortable. There are so many shysters in the world today, selling all manner of ecstasy and escapism.

Even so, what I mean to say is that rather than capitulating to word vomit or silence, there is something beautiful about offering the very elements of language as worship unto the God of all language. Our babble somehow levels the towers of Babel all over again.

We open our mouths. Sounds come out. Who can say what wonders may be seeded in these utterances? Who can fully deny this expression of the Spirit? Rainer Maria Rilke told a young poet, "Even the best err in words when they are meant to mean most delicate and almost inexpressible things."[10]

8. Emerson, *Essays*, 13.

9. Eliot, *Four Quartets*, 30.

10. Rilke, *Letters to a Young Poet*, 26.

10

Salvation

───────────

It is interesting, though rather pathetic, to note here that the success of a
certain type of Christianity depends almost wholly on this sense of guilt. For
the "gospel" will be accepted only by those in whom the sense of guilt can be
readily awakened or stimulated. Indeed, missioners of this type of Christianity (flying incidentally in the face of Christ's own example) will go all out to
induce and foster "conviction of sin" in their hearers.

—J. B. PHILLIPS

In 1951, my grandfather was touring around the South on an Indian
motorcycle, entering in local track races and generally raising Cain. He
grew up in rural Alabama, in what I imagine would be considered poor cir-
cumstances by today's standards no less than the standards of his day, but
he didn't know it. His daddy, my great grandpa Roy, was not a churchgoing
man. My grandfather had quit school after the eighth grade, so when he got
that motorbike, he left for good.

No photographs survive of my grandfather from those days, but it's
not hard to envision him on his bike. He is still a hulk of a man in his eighties today, and if he was a fighter then I don't imagine he lost too many. He
kept his Lucky Strikes rolled up in the sleeve of his white shirt and made
enough money in the local races to get to the next town. Sometimes he

stopped at farms to pick cotton, for a little eating money. You can still get a sack of boiled peanuts fresh from an iron cauldron for a few cents on the side of most any road in rural Alabama today, and that's food enough for any wanderer.

My grandfather needed a place to stay between races, so he found an uncle in Decatur, Alabama, who took him in, on one condition: he had to attend the local Pentecostal church that night. Since that seemed a small price to pay for room and board, my granddad, leather jacket and all, went along. He must have been quite a sight in those days, all six-foot-four of his commanding presence in that room full of mostly kids and old ladies, I imagine. What happened is a scene that has been replayed a thousand times in a thousand forgotten places all over the South, and a million forgotten places across the whole world. It reminds me of the arenas of Rome, where grown men took a stand of faith against all odds, and as a result the world was changed in time.

My grandfather, as we say in the South, "got saved" that night. He made a decision to surrender his entire life—past, present, and future—to the will of God. "If you confess with your mouth that Jesus is Lord," Paul writes in Romans 10:9, "and believe in your heart that God raised him from the dead, you shall be saved." He was "born again," another term we throw around to describe this commitment. All was made new.

Who knows what it was that so gripped the man in that little brick church—whatever it is that has ever gripped anyone faced with the prospect of God. John Wesley found his heart "strangely warmed" at a reading of Martin Luther's commentary on Romans, the moment he received the assurance of his salvation. Certainly nobody in that place in Alabama knew about Luther or Wesley. But they would have agreed with Luther that you don't choose spiritual salvation, salvation chooses you. In the Deep South, people still "get saved" all the time right out of God's nowhere, just cooking breakfast, driving to work, on a cigarette break and salvation just softly dawns on you, like falling into a featherbed for a nap. I read once about an alcoholic in Georgia who, drunk one night, stepped outside and thought he heard singing from the sky. That was the moment he got saved. He never once went to church after that, but never touched another drink for the rest of his life. "Being saved is more like falling in love with God," Clark Pinnock writes.[1]

1. Pinnock, *Flame of Love*, 156.

Wherever the strange warming in my granddad's heart came from, when the altar call was given for "all ye sinners to come home," he virtually ran, pouring out his tears of shame and hope on that concrete floor. I have heard him tell the story a hundred times over. His first thought when he knelt in the altar: "I don't know how to pray." So the people "prayed him through," as we say. They got him where he needed to go. He fell into the beauty of God.

A few years ago, I went with him back to that same tiny church. The entire long trip I thought he might cry like a child at any moment, but he just reminisced. He knows that he has preached to tens of thousands across the globe because of that random Sunday night service in the middle of Nowheresville, Alabama, complete with music from the red back hymnal, convicting preaching, and the very wonder of heaven itself swirling all around like holy wind.

"Strange warmth"—that's what Wesley called "gettin' saved," and Pentecostals perfected the craft of getting that warmth burned into people. You might say that we are pros at creating the "crisis moment" of faith—the instant challenge that compresses the essence of one's humanity down to a singular decision. In this decision, everything about one's life hangs in the balance. Some scientists say the energy of the cosmos was compressed to the size of the head of a pin before creation broke forth. The decision of salvation is something like that. On the pin everything about life, death, and eternity is compressed. Immense energies beckon forth. I think everyone has that moment with life and God in one way or another, and it's pretty beautiful if you think about it. "Choose you this day whom you will serve," Joshua 24:15 challenges. We choose so many things already. "As for me and my house," Joshua declares, "we will serve the LORD." For Pentecostals, the moment of this decision equals salvation.

Unfortunately, just as the Pentecostal belief in the future of creation was hijacked by escapism, some Christians have gone about making the crisis moment of faith into a head count, then an industry, which ruins the majesty of it. They have wrapped the message of salvation in a package of fear, and this is tragic.

Fear is like jet fuel. Fear will get you where you are trying to get. Some Pentecostals found out they could utilize fear better even than the government. Why? Because *fear works*. If it didn't work, the politicians wouldn't remind us of 9/11 every five minutes, and the stock market wouldn't swing on a dime. If fear didn't work, every self-help title in the bookstore wouldn't be pitching what you desperately need but won't ever have without buying a book. And if fear didn't work, plenty of the Pentecostal preachers I grew up hearing would be out of a job.

The first sermon I can recollect hearing told the story of two teenagers who wound up in hell after an auto accident caused by some sort of sinful carousing. I was at church camp, and the camp evangelist drew the story to a climax with the speed that the cops said the teens were driving ("120 miles per hour!"), as if that somehow made their fate more shocking. Needless to say, the altars were full of kids "gettin' saved" that night. Fear works.

A friend of mine has a message he still preaches to youth groups called "30 Minutes to Hell," full of multimedia elements that literally count down the seconds to the audience's eternal damnation, prior to the dramatic altar call. Teenagers always respond by praying a prayer of salvation. Fear works.

There's even a bestselling book, *23 Minutes in Hell*, detailing the cruel fate of those who miss out on God's salvation. The message of all this, and the way in which it summarizes the gospel, is simple: Jesus is a fire escape. Regardless of what he said or did, take the ticket and get the hell out of hell.

Not only does such silliness obviously cheapen God's salvation, it cheapens God's wrath, too. We tread on dangerous ground when we act as if salvation can be boiled down to some kind of quick route out of damnation. That's like trading away the diamond ring because we can't stop obsessing over the dingy case. And fear-based religion feeds on itself. Once you've reduced the gospel to a get-out-of-jail-free card, it's a short leap to casting God in a horror movie. This, of course, is exactly what Jesus was trying to talk everyone out of, and why he got laughed at a lot.

What did Jesus call his message of salvation? He called it the gospel, which means "good news." But the word is bigger than that, especially in Jesus's historical context, where there were rival gospels in play. For Jesus to claim that his good news was in fact the best news was nothing short of spiritual and political treason.

"The Spirit of the Lord is upon me," Jesus announced to his hometown synagogue back in Nazareth, to the same people who changed his diapers, wiped his snotty nose, and endured his puberty, "because he has anointed me to preach *good news* to the poor. He has sent me to proclaim freedom for the prisoners and recovery of sight for the blind, to release the oppressed, to proclaim the year of the Lord's favor" (Luke 4:18–19). The people got so angry about this reading from the Old Testament book of Isaiah that they tried to throw Jesus off a cliff, and I probably would have too if I were them. Because everyone in that backwater town knew exactly what Jesus was saying, and it sounds just as nuts today. "Today this scripture is fulfilled in your hearing," Jesus asserted, meaning that all that the people had been waiting for over the centuries was now here. God's salvation, the new age of God's reign, was dawning. And Mary's snotty-nosed boy was about to prove it to everybody.

Not only was the coming age of good news a theme in the Old Testament, it was also central to the Roman Empire's ideology. Just as our presidents love to talk about the economy, the Caesars loved to talk about the "gospel," the story of how the Roman emperors had saved the world from chaos. In the *Acts of the Divine Augustus*, the cities of Asia get together to rearrange the calendar so that the first day of the year falls on September 23—Augustus's birthday. In an inscription in the ancient city of Prienne, the cities introduce their edict by declaring that "the birthday of the god Caesar Augustus first brought to the world the gospel."[2] Just as the Old Testament prophets looked forward to the coming age of God's reign, the Caesars claimed it had arrived in Roman rule.

What's interesting is that Caesar always uses the plural form of the word, "gospels," perhaps for exaggerated impact. Jesus and his apostles use only the singular, as if to make an exclusive claim to the good news about the world's salvation. It's no wonder that the Caesars hunted them down like rats, and no wonder that the Christians didn't care much. Finding the one, true gospel of salvation has that effect on a person—it's like finding the pearl of great price. You'll mindlessly blow your whole life on it if you aren't careful.

The problem with shrinking Jesus and his gospel down to the washing of our sins, and the resultant jailbreak from hell, is that it catches only a sliver of the enormity of God's salvation—and even worse, it can cast God in the likeness of Caesar, just powering up on Jesus so that He doesn't have

2. Rice, *Paul and Patronage*, 146.

to be as cruel to the rest of us. Instead, in Jesus's gospel of salvation, a new kind of savior brings good news not by way of power over the world but by way of weakness in the face of it. My teacher, David Rhoads, writes, "God was in Christ not in order to reconcile God's self to the world. Rather, God was in Christ reconciling the world to God's self. . . . The act of God was an act of grace, done not to satisfy God but for the sake of humanity."[3]

"Do you not think I could call down two legions of angels?" Jesus asks in the Garden of Gethsemane, and this question most describes the cross of Christ as the centerpiece of his gospel. The answer to the question is not that to call down the angels would prevent him from fulfilling his mission. The point is that such a strategy of power would turn the mission inside out. Jesus's good news would sound just like Caesar's. Instead, Jesus's gospel of weakness paves a way for the weak, the powerless, the outsiders, those who do not know how to pray, to fall into beauty. "While we were still sinners, Christ died for us" (Rom 5:8).

My grandfather didn't spill the guts of his soul in that Alabama church on a Sunday night because he was terrified of impending judgment but because he was awestruck by God and goodness. That is the way of salvation, the way of the gospel. The "strange warmth" of salvation is still being felt, a warmth that says "no" to the gospels of Caesar's horror-movie God and "yes" to the fearless faith of a child, the bold way of the cross, the gospel of freedom, healing, and favor that Jesus announced in Nazareth. "If anyone is in Christ, there is a new creation," St. Paul says, and that new creation can dawn on you clear out of the blue.

---

3. Rhoads, *Challenge of Diversity*, 55.

11

The Bible

_____

O Give me that book! At any price, give me the book of God! I have it: here is knowledge enough for me. Let me be *homo unius libri*. Here then I am, far from the busy ways of men. I sit down alone: only God is here. In his presence I open, I read his book.

—JOHN WESLEY

A few years ago I preached at a Pentecostal church on the South Side of Chicago that had committed that year to reading Scripture out loud during their Sunday morning services. This is a pretty progressive thing for our movement, since slotting public readings into a Pentecostal worship service seems prefabbed. A Pentecostal who doesn't read the Bible in private is either an illiterate Pentecostal or not a Pentecostal at all. But a Pentecostal church trying out public readings is venturing into some seriously uncharted territory. Wasn't this a common liturgical element among churches that lacked the leading of the Holy Spirit?

I quickly realized that we weren't at all slipping into liturgy when the reader began the selection. Rather than handpicking nice and uplifting passages like the upscale churches that know what they're doing, this congregation simply started at Genesis 1 and read a chapter each week. I can't imagine how uncomfortable some of those weekly readings must have been: the near angel-rape of Sodom and Gomorrah, the child sacrifice of Jephthah's daughter, the almost endless genealogical material. Add to this that they read from the King James Version, translated in the year 1611, which heightened the theatrical nature of it all. Sometimes the King James Version even uses the word *piss* and, as if that weren't enough, *pisseth*. What strange things to say before the altar and the people of God.

The morning I was the visiting preacher, the Chicago congregation had made it all the way to 2 Kings 5, which is a very long chapter about a pagan named Naaman whom the prophet Elisha heals of leprosy. Like many places in the Bible, it would be great if the writer had just stopped there, but in fact the story ends with Elisha's servant trying to get rich off of Naaman's gratitude, with the result that Elisha pronounces a curse on his own servant: "The leprosy therefore of Naaman shall cleave unto thee, and unto thy seed for ever. And he went out from his presence a leper *as white* as snow." And when the minister finished pronouncing that verse, after taking some fifteen minutes to read every word of the entire meandering chapter, that congregation cheered, clapped, and praised God like they had just heard the numbers to their winning lottery tickets. I have never heard such enthusiasm over someone contracting a deadly skin disease. Was Naaman's servant a democrat?

Among scholars who study the way that Christians study the Bible, it is often said that every Christian group has a "canon within a canon." That is, the Bible is too large and complex, its edges too jagged, for anyone to construct a reasonable system of faith without zeroing in on a few key themes that are then used as lenses for the rest of it. Some examples of those lenses would be love, justice, the afterlife, and the atonement for sin. But we Pentecostals are the last holdouts of interpretive lens picking. As I often heard growing up, "We believe in the *whole* Bible, rightly divided." That is one ambitious belief, if any belief is. "The whole Bible." Open wide.

Because of this commitment to the breadth of the Bible, Pentecostals love to reclaim obscure Scriptures that everyone else has been ignoring on purpose. There are good reasons to wait until your kids are teenagers before terrifying them with the story of Noah, good reasons to wonder whether the account of God's killing all those Egyptian children and then telling His people to wipe out the Canaanites should be required reading. In the early twentieth century, a famous British novelist, Evelyn Waugh, bet Winston Churchill's son, Randolph, twenty pounds that he would tire of the Bible before reading it all the way through. Randolph started in Genesis and couldn't get enough. "He has never read any of it before and is hideously excited," Waugh related in a letter to a friend. "He keeps reading quotations aloud: 'I say I bet you didn't know this came in the Bible, "bring down my grey hairs in sorrow to the grave,"' or merely slapping his side & chortling . . ."[1] That is very irreverent, but God does find some strange things to do in the Bible.

Rather than run from the strange passages, we Pentecostals embrace them. I can't tell you the number of sermons I have heard where my first thought wasn't simply, "How is he going to make this passage say anything meaningful?" but "How did he even *find* this passage?" Like Indiana Jones exploring dangerous caves for invaluable relics, our ministers go spelunking for dark gems where no one else seems to be looking.

I heard sermons about Ehud in Judges 3, "the left-handed man" who killed a king so fat that his gut swallowed the sword whole. I heard sermons about Elisha, who caused fallen ax heads to float and called she-bears out of the woods to maul dozens of children in 2 Kings 2. I heard sermons about the conquest of the Canaanites in the book of Joshua. "Let nothing be left alive," God was fond of saying during the war effort. "The babies, the animals, run them all through." This is a part of the whole Bible, rightly divided.

I even heard sermons about Jesus that were cringe-worthy, expositions on the problematic "reproductive parts" of the woman with the issue of blood who is healed in Mark 5. If the Bible passage was freakish or gross, there was a Pentecostal sermon cooking like shortbread in it somewhere.

It was quite a surprise, given this background, when I arrived for my first graduate class at the Presbyterian seminary. It was a class on Paul's Letter to the Galatians, and we were encouraged to explore all of the options for understanding the apostle's argument. "Express what you think," the professor told us. "What do you think about what Paul is saying? How does it impact us today? Maybe Paul was wrong." No one flinched, even as I thought the ground might swallow us all up. "It's the Bible," I thought to myself. "None of it is allowed to be wrong."

1. Cited in Dawkins, *God Delusion*, 51.

By the time I got to my PhD seminars in biblical studies, I had been fed a steady diet of such smack. I studied the "historical Jesus," who wound up looking much more like my lefty hipster classmates than the mysterious foreigner of the gospels. I took a class on "postcolonial interpretation" where I learned that the violent texts of Scripture were all bad news. I remember a professor from the University of Chicago blanketing the whole Bible in this way. "The Bible on the whole is an instrument of colonization," he lectured. I can't say I disagree, but we are all colonized by something or other. Not one of us is original.

Some of these new trends are just the natural hazards of Bible study. In Chaim Potok's novel *The Promise*, a Jewish scholar teases out this tension with a rabbinical student. "How can we teach others to regard the tradition critically *and* with love? I grew up loving it, and then learned to look at it critically. That's everyone's problem today. How to love and respect what you are being taught to dissect."[2]

Most Christian traditions would easily resonate with this tension. Not Pentecostals. We shout over Naaman's leprous servant about as easily as we shout over the resurrection of Christ. It is all valid. All of it speaks. We don't dissect the biblical text, as if it were an object to be studied. We live into it, as if it were a soul. We don't read it so much as it reads us.

I once heard a famous biblical scholar say in a lecture, "We all live by a script, be it explicit or implicit." Stories, not external propositions or innate drives, are the raw materials of our consciousness. Many people are driven by the story of independence and the American dream: *more plus better equals life*. Many people are driven by the story of promise-filled romantic love, which fuels the top forty Billboard hits: *I can be completed by someone else, who will make all of my unhappiness happy*. Some are driven by hedonism: *Eat, drink and be merry, for tomorrow we die*. Unfortunately, the latter option is the most popular—the script of our present age of militaristic conquest and technological consumerism.

Few persons are intentional about the script of their lives, at least in the West. We allow our scripts to be chosen for us, yet we commit to them with all the care of a method actor. We play our parts out like the German national soccer team—no deviation, no creativity. Scripts are why everyone is the same in the suburbs. The usual life-scripts are so boring.

2. Potok, *Promise*, 298.

It is a beautiful thing that against this colorless landscape of bland top forty stories, Pentecostals choose the Bible as their script. After all, it isn't called "Scripture" for nothing. Maybe we don't know how to work with everything that is in the Bible, but it has to be better than the cultural scripts. The word is inspired by God, warts and all, so we take the risk.

Many Christians want to change Scripture, of course. They are uncomfortable with the uncomfortable parts. They create fancy arguments to make the God of the Bible a nicer, more stable deity. "The problem with the Canaanites was their sin. They deserved to die." "God let David and Solomon have all those concubines so that the messianic lineage might be preserved." Or—the worst—"The Bible is a book of the progressive revelation of God's identity. Everything was fuzzy and choppy in the early books." To each of these I say, *not so fast*. Let's not sacrifice reality for symmetry. It says what it says.

In the end, the Bible is a good script, a serious script. It is violent, unfair, and glorious. It is like life. The Bible refracts us, reflects us. It tears us to pieces only to rebuild us again. It makes us afraid of God, and rightly so. It helps us love God, which is all miracle. The Bible, in the words of Paul Tillich, "does not give us an easy comfort about ourselves."[3] We are the ones murdering the Canaanite babies in the name of God. We are the ones forgiving our neighbor. We are the prodigal son with the pigs, and we are his risk-averse older brother. We are the Good Samaritan and we are the man in the ditch. We are the lawyer who asks Jesus the question that provokes the story.

3. Tillich, *Shaking of the Foundations*, 67.

12

Evangelism

The bells say: we have spoken for centuries from the towers of great Churches. We have spoken to the saints your fathers, in their land. We called them, as we call you, to sanctity. What is the word with which we called them? We did not merely say, "Be good, come to Church." We did not merely say "Keep the commandments" but above all, "Christ is risen, Christ is risen!" And we said: "Come with us, God is good, salvation is not hard, His love has made it easy!" And this, our message, has always been for everyone, for those who came and for those who did not come, for our song is perfect as the Father in heaven is perfect and we pour our charity out upon all.

—THOMAS MERTON

When you see them coming, you batten down the hatches. Close the blinds! Put the kids in the basement! They pull into the cul-de-sac on their bicycles, stacks of blue books filling the metal baskets. Who wears a tie with a short-sleeved shirt anymore? And a name tag?

I cannot turn them away when they arrive. I do not have it in me to hide. Their success rate must be dreadfully low. I always invite them in. I read the passages from their holy book that they instruct me to read. I cannot and will not bring myself to tell them that I'm a Pentecostal minister and I think their "Second Testament to Jesus Christ" is problematic. I am too impressed with their zeal to argue with the lads. I am not interested in their theology, but I am interested in them.

They are willing to put themselves out there. They are willing to be freaks. They are willing to fail. No wonder they now regularly find themselves in halls of power everywhere. One of them was almost elected President of the United States.

You know who it is that I am describing: teenage Mormons on a mission from God. What is their mission? To convert you to their cause. Because of this mission, I feel kindred with them. Our movements are unapologetically evangelistic.

࿐

Pentecostals are not as likely to go from door to door like traveling salesmen. Our evangelistic efforts are more group-oriented. Nowhere is this better displayed than in our practice of mission trips, during which a group of us converges on a place to share the gospel in churches, streets, and markets. While spring breakers from across the country tear into Panama City and Daytona Beach to carouse and loot, Pentecostal teenagers spend the same week barnstorming hapless villages and ghettos everywhere with our message.

There was always formal training for our mission trips. We learned to share our testimony of coming to faith in Christ before practice groups. We learned attentiveness to cultural distinctives and taboos. We learned the right questions to ask to start conversations about God. We learned to make a pitch, to ask grave and eternal questions like it was the most natural thing in the world. "Do you know where you will go when you die?" I once sat through a training class where we were instructed to ask that question of the barber who would give us our next haircut. We weren't much for small talk.

I was fifteen years old when I was sent on my first mission trip to the streets of Miami, Florida. Someone stationed me in the middle of a popular street in South Beach and put a clipboard in my hand. I was given a companion, another fifteen-year-old, a girl with blonde hair who never said anything at all. It was all on me.

Armed with my list of questions, scared out of my mind, I got to work. "Who do you think God is?" "How do you think we can find God?" "Do you know about Jesus?" I heard all sorts of responses: "God is the sun." "No thank you." "I am from Holland." "Screw off." "Here's my business card. Stop by sometime."

Any parent in their right mind would stop and think about this arrangement: throwing teenagers alone into the streets of a huge city. Yet for us, mission trips were liminal spaces—rites of passage where we learned to stand on our own two feet and cold cock total strangers with a message about their eternal destiny. We Pentecostals don't make any bones about our desire to proselytize. It is who we are. It is what we do. Like the Mormons, we train our evangelists young.

I saw a movie once about a group of budding stockbrokers whose job was to chase down new sales leads. They were trained to play the sales call like a game of cat and mouse, letting the customer nibble the bait a bit. If the customer demanded to buy right then and there, however, the stockbroker would shout out to the entire room, "Reco!" That would call the pros in to reel in the big one.

Our evangelistic enterprises occasionally scored a "Reco" moment. Every so often someone would take the bait. We were trained to sniff out this possibility like a bloodhound, then to zero in for the kill. If we could get them to pray the sinner's prayer, our evangelistic work was done.

> "Repeat after me: Lord Jesus, I confess that I am a sinner deserving of hell. I thank you that you died on the cross and rose from the dead to save me and to secure me a place with you in heaven. I accept you now as my personal Lord and savior. Amen."

Notch one on the clipboard; we scored. "Reco!" Let heaven and earth rejoice. "I say unto you, that likewise joy shall be in heaven over one sinner that repenteth, more than over ninety and nine just persons, which need no repentance" (Luke 15:7).

At the end of our mission trip, the notches would be tallied up like dry goods and announced to our congregation back home, our crowning achievement. "As a result of our efforts, 87 souls were won to the Lord!" "87 people plundered from hell to populate heaven!" "Had we not followed the Lord's command to go and preach to all nations, 87 immortals would still be as lost as a goose in high weeds! But now they are found! They were blind but now they see!"

Sure, assigning souls a numerical value seems a little hokey. A prominent Presbyterian pastor made fun of us: "Those who are satisfied with merely proclaiming the Gospel and receiving professions are like immoral

seducers."[1] That is a bit strong. For us, the most moral thing in the world is
to seduce.

❧

We now live in a Western culture in which pluralism threatens to drown
out great voices. The most famous art installation in the world presently
adorns the Panthéon in Paris. Built in the eighteenth century by Louis XV,
the Panthéon, originally a church, now holds the remains of France's greatest luminaries: Voltaire, Victor Hugo, Marie Curie, and others. The inscription above the door reads, "For the Great Men." Now, however, instead of
representing a sanctuary of true greats, the French government has com-
missioned a graffiti artist to post thousands of random "selfie" photographs
all over the structure. I suppose the idea is that anyone can achieve greatness, but it is a stretch, to say the least. The truer message: there are no great
voices anymore. This message is the ultimate demolition of civilization,
democracy, and certainly of Christianity.

Pentecostals believe in greats and greatness. We believe in great voices—that some voices are greater than others, that one voice matters most
of all. This is our starting point. "I am the way, the truth, and the life," Jesus
said (John 14:6). This is why we can be so confrontational.

The challenge we face, of course, is to hang on to this passion for our
message without resorting to certitudes, exclusivism, arrogance, and trium-
phalism. But we do this quite naturally. Rather than debating in the abstract
within the cultural marketplace of ideas, we keep our evangelism personal.
It is not about ideas; it is about individuals. So we stand on the corners with
our clipboards, in coffeehouses over conversations, behind pulpits, relentless. We think—we *know*—that this stuff can change your life. It's not a sales
pitch. The whole world hangs in the balance.

"All authority in heaven and on earth has been given to me," Jesus
charges his disciples in the so-called Great Commission of evangelism.
"Therefore go and make disciples of all nations, baptizing them in the name
of the Father and of the Son and of the Holy Spirit, and teaching them to
obey everything I have commanded you" (Matt 28:18–20). There is hardly
a Pentecostal who could not quote this commission. Less remembered,
however, is the state of Jesus's addressees in the preceding verse. "When
they saw him, they worshiped him, and they doubted."

---

1. Kennedy, *Evangelism Explosion*, 103.

Perhaps it is that verse that gives us the space we need to locate ourselves on a proper evangelistic mission, a posture that includes both worship and doubt. Rather than counteract their doubt with dogma and certitudes, Jesus sends them out on mission anyway. Doubt was not a problem; it was the pathway of proselytizing. Mark Allen Powell writes, "The church in Matthew is a community of worshipping doubters, and they always make the best evangelists. We can only testify to Jesus as people who do not have it all together, as people whose lives are still a bit of a mess."[2]

Surely that is the kind of evangelism that we Christians can all buy into. As long as I can remain something of a mess, maybe I will buy a bicycle with a metal basket in the front and a short-sleeved shirt. Maybe I will map out my town, clip a name tag onto my tie and give the Mormons a run for their money. "Repeat after me . . ."

---

2. Powell, *Loving Jesus*, 124–25.

13

Relevance

The gospel and its communication present to every culture a "challenging relevance." It is relevant insofar as it is embodied in terms by which people of the culture have learned to understand their world. It is challenging in that in every culture, Jesus is introduced as one who bursts open the culture's models with power of a wholly new fact.

—GEORGE HUNSBERGER

Growing up in the South, pretty much every kid goes to youth group, at least until they can drive and have a choice in the matter. Youth group is our traditional term for an intentional teenage gathering at a church. They usually meet on a weeknight: Wednesday or Friday. In more sophisticated circles, the youth group has given way to the fancier "student ministry," but the difference between these two things can't be overstated.

As a high school kid, I visited a big Baptist "student ministry" once on a Friday night in a nice suburb of Atlanta. It was like an MTV set crossed with an ESPN Zone. They had a ton of kids, all white and preppy, with free pizza, entertaining games, great bands, and a smooth-talking youth pastor who didn't say anything that wasn't at least fairly cool. There wasn't a bit of pressure to respond to the sermon, which I wasn't used to. It was like they had done a focus group with teenagers in the mall and built a rather unreligious religious experience just for them. Although I liked the student ministry, it made about as much sense to me as building a pizza parlor and then serving fried chicken.

I knew through my friends that these student ministries were really excited about partnering with parents to raise responsible, and at least semi-Christian, kids. They were pretty lightweight on the spiritual stuff in their approach, but they had lots of seminars on parenting strategies and encouraged students to listen to positive music and took the upperclassmen to Daytona Beach for a tamer version of spring break each year. They may as well have been the college Republicans.

In Pentecostal youth group, there weren't very many cool kids, and there wasn't much in the way of pizza or seminars or beach trips either. No focus groups went into getting it together. We did have snazzy Christian T-shirts with slogans about burning in hell ("Turn or Burn!"), but other than that it was just our traditional Pentecostal spirituality served up raw.

The summer before my freshman year of high school, my family moved to a new Pentecostal church in a rough area of town with about a hundred people in attendance. The church began to grow, and we were able to hire our first youth minister. One might think that such a step could lead us toward the goal of a successful, über-cool "student ministry." Not a chance.

Our youth pastor hailed from the mountains of Virginia, so there wasn't anything "cool" about him. He had cut off one of his fingers in shop class, and almost lost one of his feet to a lawn mower, so he made you nervous right off the bat. He had a mustache. He often preached to us with a big stick in his hand, like a nun with a ruler, so he could strike our chairs when he became excited or enraged. He was a force of nature. His youth ministry mantra was simple and oh-so-Pentecostal: "We are not here to have fun. We are here to meet with God. Get in or get out."

And meet we did. While all the hip student ministries went on social outings, our youth group had Tuesday night prayer meetings. While the student ministries had slick concerts, our youth group had worship. While the student ministries had weekend ski trips, our youth group had weekend "retreats" with worship services morning, noon, and night. While the student ministries had social outings, our youth group went downtown to hang out with the homeless. While the student ministries had exciting summer camps at the beach, our youth group took "mission trips" to God-forsaken places. When I was fifteen, our big summer youth trip was to a small church in Appalachia. Our agenda: reroof the church in one hundred degree weather. Every morning at six, my youth minister would walk into the church basement, where we were sleeping on the floor, and kick us in the ribs: "On the roof in five minutes!" he barked. I raised money to have experiences like this.

My youth group defied the common logic about how churches should attract families. My youth group certainly defied what many assume they know about teenagers. And our approach worked, dramatically.

My youth minister created an entirely new organization for like-minded youth workers who wanted to follow his no-fun approach. After a few years of banding together with other Pentecostal youth groups, we had an impressive assemblage of several hundred teenagers. At our week-end retreats, we even had over a thousand. Imagine a crowd of hormone-drenched, sugar-and-caffeine-addled teenagers gathered together within the expressed rubric that no fun will be had: no games, no icebreakers, no recreation, no free time, nothing. Trying to describe that kind of Pentecostal youth group to outsiders is like trying to describe some lost pygmy culture to someone who has never been outside the Georgia state lines.

Youth groups in which that kind of energy is directed away from fun and toward God Himself are bound to be a sight to behold. One fairly un-stable lady in our church was so moved by the sight of hundreds of teenagers with their hands raised in fervent worship that she ran to the church office and dialed up, of all places, the fire department. "There's kids on fire at our church!" she preached into the phone. They must have sent every fire truck in the county blazing into our parking lot. Firemen in helmets, oxygen tanks and full astronaut gear burst through the doors in the middle of our worship service. We stopped worshipping and all stared at one an-other, attempting to interpret the scene. After a few minutes they left; we shrugged our shoulders and resumed worshipping. Just another night at youth group.

"If you ask almost any adult about the impact of church school on his or her growth," Walter Brueggemann writes, "he or she will not tell you about books or curriculum or Bible stories or anything like that. The central memory is of the teacher; learning is *meeting*."[1] Yes, this is what I remember most, the *meeting* of it all. "All actual life is encounter," Martin Buber wrote.[2]

I loved the meeting, the encounter of it. I loved it all. Pentecostal youth group became something of my primary identity. I didn't want to play sports. I didn't want to get involved at school. I wanted to smoke what my youth minister was pushing. I bought it all—hook, line, and sinker. And believe me when I tell you that it was beautiful, both then and in memoriam now. A lovely time of life.

I remember power-spraying a wall of some slum in downtown Miami that we were cleaning up on a weeklong "missions trip," chips of leaded paint covering me head to toe. And all by myself, with the sprayer going full blast, I felt a conversion wash over me just as though I'd walked a Baptist aisle, like a Holy Ghost pressure-washing. "If this is Christianity," I remember clearly thinking to myself, "I'm in."

I remember sitting with a homeless man downtown on a Friday night when our youth group was feeding the homeless. As he chain-smoked cigarettes I joined him on the curb, and we held a one-on-one conversation for over an hour, even as I strained to understand his dialect and to withstand his odor. We talked about God, and whether smoking tobacco was a sin, and about heaven and hell. "I'm all in," I thought as he chatted away.

I remember the roof of Appalachia as the rising sun burned the fog off the ground, the impression of a foot in my ribs, sweat pouring everywhere. I remember straightening out rows of shingles, as a Catholic priest presents the host, offering them to God. "Let us build a cathedral so great that those who follow will think us mad for having made the attempt," reads an inscription in Seville Cathedral, the largest in the world. That Spanish cathedral took more than a century to complete. "Let us roof a church in the mountains of Virginia with a bunch of teenagers." It took us just one week, yet it felt like painting the Sistine Chapel.

I remember what seem now like a thousand raucous worship services, standing in the center of the action. Sometimes I felt nothing. Sometimes I felt ecstasy running through my blood, visions in my head ("I know a man who visited the third heaven," Paul says in 2 Cor 12:2). It was all so effortless and home. It didn't matter what was going on, either in the service or inside of me. I was just in, regardless of anything or anyone. I was just all in.

1. Brueggemann, *Living Toward a Vision*, 167.

2. Buber, *I and Thou*, 62.

How does all this sound to you? Imbalanced and extreme, like a brain-washing? Like indoctrination into a cult? I can see why you might draw such conclusions, but they are all wrong.

❧

Something Pentecostals have seemed to intuitively understand is that the concept of *relevance* is in the eye of the beholder. If you live in a place where there are no roads, donkeys are terrifically relevant. If you live in the penthouse suite, elevators make perfect sense. So if you move from the penthouse to the farm, or vice versa, an overhaul of relevance takes place. If you are a preppy white kid from the suburbs, a church student ministry experience that feels like a stroll through Abercrombie and Fitch is relevant. If you are a Pentecostal, you probably aren't anything like that kid (and you may hate him and all his friends). My youth minister essentially gave us permission, then, to redefine relevance, to accept the new reality all around. To cite *The Matrix*, "There is no spoon."

This redefinition is exactly what we see happening in the New Testament.

Scott Bartchy teaches at UCLA, and he has spent most of his career tackling the question of early Christian re-socialization. How did a movement based on the cult of a crucified Jewish peasant convince upstanding folks who had never even met a Jew that *most everything they had ever thought about the world was irrelevant*? We tend to call such a decisive moment "conversion," but in our society this concept is relegated to the private sphere. When most of us convert, we have less to unlearn. For first-century peoples to accept the gospel as truth meant that all of the cognitive building blocks they had used to construct their priorities, values, and inner worlds were wrong. Caesar wasn't god. Idols weren't real. Temples and priests weren't necessary. All this was crazy talk back then, and Jesus and St. Paul were the chief crazymakers.

"The historical-Jesus traditions and the writings of Paul both share and emphasize the same radical reversals of core traditional cultural values,"[3] Bartchy contends. In the words of New Testament scholar Edwin Judge a generation ago, this radical reversal of values occurred "in violent reaction to much that was central to the classical way of life."[4] For Christianity to get off the ground, there had to be a small group of people willing to live

3. Bartchy, "Who Should Be Called Father?," 146.
4. Judge, "St. Paul and Classical Culture," 19.

counter-culturally, to deconstruct relevance and go "all in" to irrelevance. My friend Brian Tucker at Moody Bible Institute calls this "the formation of social identity."[5]

"From now on those who have wives should live as if they had none; those who mourn, as if they did not; those who are happy, as if they were not; those who buy something, as if it were not theirs to keep; those who use the things of the world, as if not engrossed in them." Paul says this to a new congregation in Greek Corinth, radically redefining what is relevant and what is not. "For this world in its present form is passing away" (1 Cor 7:29–31). Marriage, happiness, possessions—all irrelevant, he says. Abercrombie, fun, cool: they are all passing away.

Perhaps it is this renegotiation of reality that makes Pentecostalism a global youth movement demographically, while many of our other Protestant congregations are aging out. "One can have life-changing meetings that open one to new kinds of existence," Brueggemann continues. "And that surely is what church education must be about." Cultural irrelevance has never been so relevant.

5. Tucker, *You Belong to Christ*, 1.

14

Mystery

Mysticism keeps men sane. As long as you have mystery you have health; when you destroy mystery you create morbidity. The ordinary man has always been sane because the ordinary man has always been a mystic. He has permitted the twilight. He has always had one foot in earth and the other in fairyland.

—G. K. CHESTERTON

My favorite author is Frederick Buechner, a Presbyterian minister now in his eighties. I think he is a Presbyterian on the outside because he has a respectable Ivy League background. On the inside, I'm convinced, he's a wild-eyed Pentecostal. I've never encountered a writer who embraced erratic, holy mystery with such anti-expert abandon.

Buechner's road to faith and ministry did not begin early in his life. His father took his own life when Frederick was a child and his mother and grandparents were run-of-the-mill atheists in New England. Although, as a writer, Buechner was inwardly disposed, he never thought of God. God was simply never introduced in his family. Like his father's suicide, no one spoke of the subject.

In 1950, his senior year at Princeton University, Buechner took a summer away to complete his first novel, *A Long Day's Dying*. The book was an immediate and smashing success in literary circles, propelling him to great commercial and professional success. He was hailed by *Time*, *Newsweek*, and the major book reviews as America's next great novelist—at the ripe old age of twenty-four.

And so he did what America's next great novelist does. He moved to New York City, published in the *New Yorker*, became a lecturer at New York University, and squeezed every drop of excitement out of life as a young, prominent bachelor. In the 1950s, however, the city that never sleeps did tend to take a nap on Sunday mornings—the one morning on which there was not that much to do in Manhattan. Buechner walked out of his brownstone and happened to notice that he lived beside the historic Madison Avenue Presbyterian Church. He started attending in order to hear the preacher, whom he had heard about: George Buttrick, perhaps the most famous active preacher in America at the time.

After attending for several months of Sundays, Buechner came to appreciate Buttrick's cadence. The preacher was serious, but not overly so, and a fine storyteller. One fateful morning, Buttrick opened his sermon with an event that everyone had been buzzing about—the recent coronation of Elizabeth II at Westminster Abbey. His text was the temptation of Jesus in the wilderness, and with his trademark eloquence, Buttrick described the way that Jesus was offered a crown by Satan, a coronation right then and there in the wilderness, which he refused. Buttrick said Jesus refused that coronation so that he might be crowned as king in each of our hearts—crowned among confession, crowned among tears, and—a phrase that would change Buechner's life forever—crowned among *"great laughter."*

Buechner writes in his memoir,

> Jesus is crowned among confession and tears and great laughter, and at the phrase "great laughter," for reasons that I have never satisfactorily understood, the great wall of China crumbled and Atlantis rose up out of the sea, and on Madison Avenue, at 73rd Street, tears leapt from my eyes as though I had been struck across the face.[1]

Sometime later, after attending Union Theological Seminary in New York City, being ordained as a Presbyterian minister, and continuing his writing career, Buechner obtained the manuscript that George Buttrick had

1. Buechner, *Alphabet of Grace*, 44.

preached from that day. When he surfed to the place in the manuscript that had catalyzed his conversion, all the words were there, except for the phrase that broke his heart.

Did the preacher improvise upon his usually wooden manuscript, inspired in an instant to let loose that fateful phrase? Or was the phrase "and great laughter" one that Frederick Buechner heard but that George Buttrick never spoke?

"We are talking about God," St. Augustine announced in a sermon a millennium and a half ago. "What wonder is it that you do not understand? If you do understand, then it is not God."[2] This is the God that Pentecostals know best, a clever deity. He sneaks around putting words into people's mouths, into people's ears, wooing them to places they may or may not want to go.

⁂

For Pentecostals, God is a God of mystery. That is exactly what the world needs these days.

I do not have to tell you that we live in a mystery-averse society. Turn on the television, visit the local Barnes and Noble, pay for any manner of daylong seminar, and you'll find a host of preachers, self-help gurus, and politicians who have figured out the meaning of life on your behalf. Just vote for this party, or buy this book, or join this fitness plan and you'll have the life of your dreams, exactly as it was meant to be. The experts have met together and decided what works. They have answered Pontius Pilate's eternal question, "What is truth?" It is all 100 percent guaranteed.

One might hope that churches would stand as bastions against this kind of arrogant certainty, but this is rarely the case. In fact, one of the fastest-growing segments of theological thought in America might be called the "neo-Reformed" movement. Reformed theology is originally associated with John Calvin, who championed the idea that God preselects people for eternal life or eternal damnation, thus marginalizing the role of human free will and decision-making. The new face of Calvinism is reflected in a host of large, young, white churches associated with this outlook, and it is not difficult to see why. They pose as hipsters (a seminal article on the movement is titled "Young, Restless, and Reformed"[3]), but in reality

2. Cited in Dillard, *For the Time Being*, 47. See also Bradshaw, "Augustine the Metaphysician," 245.

3. Hanson, "Young, Restless, and Reformed," 32–38.

they are fundamentalists who believe they have everything figured out, or God has figured everything out on their behalf. In the words of New Testament scholar Scot Mcknight, "the NeoReformed have come to equate the meaning of 'gospel' with Calvin's 'Reformed theology.' And those who aren't Reformed are somehow or in some ways denying the gospel itself."[4]

This neo-Reformed fundamentalism does not only include who is selected for salvation. It includes all kinds of other exclusions. Miracles? Check "ended with the death of the apostles." Women? Check "not allowed to lead anything in church except the nursery." Who are our enemies? Check "anyone who does not agree with us."

Certitudes are attractive. People are drawn to them. They are attractive because they so quickly replace God. They are easier to understand and easier to get along with. And so some Christians suck the pure mystery right out of faith, like siphoning a gas tank.

In contrast, Pentecostals readily embrace mystery. We embrace what the ancient Celts called "thin places"—places where the membrane separating the heavens from the earth breaks down, and holy mystery breaks forth. Miracles happen all around—extraordinary and ordinary. I have seen people break into fits of laughter while praying at the altar. Did they perceive the mystery in a thin place? I have heard stories of literal pillars of fire appearing above car windshields to lead ordinary people through dangerous weather, reminiscent of Israel's exodus from Egypt. You just never know. Craig Keener, a Methodist scholar who teaches at Asbury Seminary, wrote a definitive two-volume work on miracles when he married an African Pentecostal and suddenly encountered people who claimed to have seen folk resurrected from the dead. Such are our stories, our Pentecostal mysteries.

"I pray also that the eyes of your heart may be enlightened," Paul told the Ephesians, "in order that you may know the hope to which he has called you, the riches of his glorious inheritance in the saints, and his incomparably great power for us who believe" (1:18–19). Paul prays for the vision of the heart, the vision of orientation. Was Paul not praying that we might perceive the unperceivable, that we might be exposed to the mystery of God and live through it? Through the centuries, Christian teachers have referred to God as the *mysterium tremendum et fascinans*, "the great mystery

4. McKnight, "Who Are the NeoReformed? 2," par. 2.

and fascination" that attracts and repels us.[5] Is this not more reasonable than neo-Reformed FAQ sheets?

At twenty-two years old I encountered the *mysterium tremendum* in the poorest place I have ever been to. I was halfway through my degree at (a Reformed!) seminary and less than a year into my first job in ministry, serving as a part-time youth minister. Our church had made some connections with a missionary family in Nicaragua, one of the most poverty-stricken countries in the western hemisphere, and I was able to lead my first mission trip that summer with a dozen high school students. On the last day of the trip, the missionary told us that he wanted us to meet someone: an elderly lady named Miss Ruby.

He didn't say much about Miss Ruby, just that she stayed at home most of the time, but from her house she held Pentecostal prayer meetings and worship services, preaching to whomever might show up. As our group drove toward her neighborhood, I was getting legitimately nervous for our safety. She lived in a massive slum. Unemployment in Nicaragua is so high that the neighborhoods are filled with men, especially young men, who often have to resort to crime and street warfare in order to survive. People were walking up to our van and checking us out. When I think about that van ride, images of Somalia come to mind. It seemed like we were driving further and further into pure, ungovernable chaos. I was scared.

Finally we made it to the home, the shack that we were looking for; Miss Ruby was standing outside. She was one of the shortest people I have encountered. She had lost many of her teeth and wore an old dress with her dark hair pulled back. She looked both ancient and full of life, like a sensei. She spoke pretty good English, which was itself mysterious. Why would anyone living in that neighborhood need to speak English? She invited us in.

The house did have a roof and electricity, and the front room was big enough for our group to uncomfortably pile into. She was very welcoming, even as none of us really knew what we would be doing there. As if the scene couldn't get any stranger, Miss Ruby pulled out a guitar, sat on a chair, and started singing Pentecostal worship songs that we knew in English. We all sang along. Then she opened the Bible and she shared something. I cannot remember what it was. But what happened next I would not believe if I had not been there.

5. Long, *Twentieth-Century Western Philosophy*, 148.

Miss Ruby began to go around our circle and pray for each one of us, one by one. These prayers were not general; they were so specific that I was trembling. Before she prayed for one in our circle she would ask questions about them. "Young man, how long have you been adopted?" "Young lady, why do you question your husband's love for you? He has special love for you." "Young man, why do you fear all the day long?"

She went person to person that way, revealing an awareness of their situation back home that was absolutely hair-raising. I was the last one to be prayed for, so I had plenty of time to stress over whether or not I had any secrets that were about to be outed to the whole gathering in her living room. And when she came to me, like the Delphic oracle of the ancient world, she told me things buried deep within my heart. She told me exactly what I was there in that slum to hear.

"Where can I go from your Spirit?" the psalmist asks. "Why do people in churches seem like cheerful, brainless tourists on a packaged tour of the Absolute?"[6] Annie Dillard asks. "What kind of uncategorized mystery is this?" I ask. Who is this Pentecostal God, sneaking around, putting words into people's mouths, into their ears, wooing them to places they may or may not want to go?

6. Dillard, *Teaching a Stone to Talk*, 52.

15

Theology

Jim unwrapped his bedroll holding all his worldly wealth. There was a hat and some fruit, a pair of socks, a rabbit's foot, and a book. "What'd you bring a book for?' asked Huck with a little irritation. "T'read," said Jim with great seriousness, looking into the night. "What kinda book is it?" Huck asked. "Book 'bout theology," Jim said, his voice trailing away. "Theology? I hate theology almost as much as I hate schools and rules," Huck said, and emphasized the point by spitting into the river. "What good is a theology book on a trip like this?" Jim was silent for a long time before he answered. "Trip like this is long. Lotta things going to happen. Might come in handy."

—MARK TWAIN, *HUCKLEBERRY FINN*

Everyone who grew up Pentecostal is united by a single universal truth: all of us were mortally terrified of bringing a friend to church. We reserved sleepovers for Fridays, and if we accidentally scheduled one for a Saturday, we did whatever was necessary to get our friend out of the house before our parents invited them to "worship with us." If a friend asked about our church, we changed the subject. Even at a young age, we knew that our friends might not be able to handle our worship services, and we didn't want to scar them for life. As a youth pastor, I inadvertently took a group of uninitiated teens to a Pentecostal youth camp service. Under the power of the Spirit, some campers spontaneously fell to the ground at the altar. A poor kid from the city looked at me in horror and asked, "He dead?" I had forgotten the Pentecostal kid's cardinal rule that you don't forget the universal truth: if you want to keep your friends, by all means keep them out of your church. There is no use going around scaring people.

But adhering to the universal truth isn't as simple as it seems. It's almost like the adults had caught on to our circle of trust, and therefore waged an immense propaganda war in the service of getting us to invite friends to church. There were cash giveaways on a per-friend basis. There were "friend days." The youth minister would shave his head if we brought a certain number of friends, or the pastor would eat lunch on the church roof. We tried, of course, to find friends from other Pentecostal churches to satiate this appetite for such promotions, but that pool was sparse. I don't remember how the other kids dealt with it, but I know that I almost never brought a friend to church. The adults may have been on to us, but I was on to them. Seeing the pastor on the roof was simply no substitute for putting your friend in an environment where he might involuntarily relieve his bladder.

Even so, it was inevitable that sooner or later guilt or the promotional campaigns or the Holy Ghost would get ahold of my heart and I'd "give in to the unction of the Spirit," as folks used to say. But who was I supposed to invite? In elementary school I played with a friend in our neighborhood who was a Mormon. I didn't know what that was really, but I did think it invalidated him as a candidate. In junior high, I figured I'd take a bold leap by wearing a T-shirt with Jesus on it, but this just made me a spectacle. One of my friends thought it was the famous WWF wrestler Hulk Hogan; another sang the whole chorus to "Amazing Grace" when he saw me in the hall. None of this gave me the boldness that my Sunday school teacher told me I was supposed to have. Although I was supposed to be "not ashamed of the gospel," just like St. Paul in Romans 1, I never wore that shirt again. So much for my evangelistic exploits.

In high school the campaign didn't get any easier, even as I was buying into the idea that "people need the Lord," as one of our songs said. Again, *which* people was the question. My homecoming queen girlfriend's daddy was a successful lawyer, and even though they were churchgoing folk, they went to a church where they printed out a weekly bulletin and everyone remained calm. Their church had a stringed orchestra, for heaven's sake. I once made the mistake of bringing her to a Wednesday night youth meeting at my church, and our song leader danced like a fat King David all over the platform. After that, I figured it was in the interests of our relationship to stick to visiting her church every now and then. And I liked the orchestra.

Even the fact that my high school was a Christian school didn't help me round up a following to my church. A couple of Methodist guys who were popular made it their goal to denounce speaking in tongues as heresy to my face in our Bible class. I actually told them that I could speak in tongues right then and there if they wanted to settle the issue, which felt good to say but didn't score me any points as a witness for the Lord. Not my finest moment, but at least I didn't beat the crap out of them like I wanted to.

Despite these failures, as high school wore on I slowly turned up the heat as an evangelist for my theology. I started wearing Christian T-shirts with warnings about hell printed on them. I raised money for poor people in Bangladesh, telling the student body in a speech that they could pretty much go to the hell advertised on my T-shirt if they didn't care enough about Bangladesh to give me five bucks. In another campaign speech for the student body elections, I declared that we ought to take the name "Christian" off the sign of our school until we got ourselves in line with Scripture and did away with dress codes. (When a teacher gave me a demerit for having my shirt untucked, I quoted 1 Samuel 16:7, "Man looks at the outward appearance. The LORD looks at the heart." He seemed dumbfounded but still unconvinced.) I declared to everyone I could that the only reasonable candidate in the 1996 Republican primary for a Christian to vote for was Pat Buchanan. Incredibly, none of this rhetoric made anybody want to go to church with me. I even asked a kid with a terrible speech impediment point blank, and he said he was busy. While this betrayal of the universal truth from my childhood won me the student body vice presidency by virtue of my blazing speeches, something we Pentecostals are naturally good at, I was by all indications considered just short of a lunatic by most. Nobody wanted to come to my church.

Finally, I found my prey. And not just one—two kids accepted my invitation to church. Wouldn't you know it, they weren't the Methodist snobs or the dress code preps or the privileged kids like my girlfriend. I found two kids whom everybody made fun of. One was slow and supposedly admitted once that he only had one testicle, which didn't set him up for popularity.

The other is now openly gay, which I assumed, but saying so back then would have gotten him in trouble with everybody. These guys were so embarrassing all the way around that I finally didn't feel embarrassed bringing them to church. And both of them liked my church a lot.

Up until the present generation, it was debatable whether Pentecostals really had a distinct theology to call our own. Now many fancy things are written. For me, though, that entire story sums up Pentecostal theology.

It is hard to overestimate the profound impact of embarrassment on a life, especially a young one. After high school, I went on to study theology in college and graduate school, eventually earning a PhD. But why? Lately I've begun to think that my passionate pursuit of theological education was really a veiled attempt to emerge from the embarrassment of my Pentecostal background. I figured my Mormon playmate was hellbound, but he went to "temple" and could expound on the precise doctrines of his church, and it amazed me. I hated those Methodist boys for mocking me, but they knew things that Martin Luther and John Wesley had said and I wanted to be like them. If the alternative was to hang out with gay outcasts and losers with one testicle, sign me up for the orchestra church.

I wanted a theology. I wanted to be able to articulate it. I wanted to be smart and debonair, not embarrassed.

Getting a college degree helped some, but it was a Pentecostal university. I needed more. I enrolled in a Presbyterian seminary, the liberal and prestigious kind of Presbyterian, for graduate school. I wanted to learn what exactly theology was, first of all, and then embrace one that didn't embarrass me.

I got a scholarship for the master's program since I was a Pentecostal and didn't have any money, which made it hard to hide my identity. I met all kinds of smart people and I was suspicious of nearly all of them. Teachers often went out of their way to include me, which was embarrassing. "Josh, how does *your tradition* approach theology?" *Your tradition.* I went there in the first place to get away from embarrassment, and I was singled out all the time.

There was one conversation, though, in which I actually surprised myself. It's rare that we blurt out things that we didn't even know we had discovered, but for whatever reason my guard was down and I admitted, more to myself than to anyone else, exactly what I was doing at that esteemed Presbyterian school. I was searching for a theology.

My scholarship required that I work a certain number of hours at the seminary, and they put me in some back room in the library sticking hard plastic covers on paperback books. Initially they tried to put me in the cafeteria, but I only lasted a day before requesting a different job. I couldn't handle all the fawning Presbyterians wanting me to feel comfortable and cheery about scooping their gravy.

At my request they transferred me to solitary confinement among the newly received collections in the bowels of the library, which suited me fine. Occasionally, a guy my age worked with me. He had a patchy, unmanaged beard that I think he grew for intellectual reasons, even though it made him look like a hobo. He definitely thought he was smart, and he probably was, and perhaps he meant the beard to be some kind of external indicator of this fact.

Since we worked together on the book covers, one day I asked him about himself, and he made reference to his Presbyterian upbringing and his goal to teach theology for a living. He asked me about my background, I told him about it, and an awkward silence ensued. For a moment, it was like I was a specimen in a zoo, like he had never seen a real live Pentecostal. Since it was just the two of us staring back at each other in that big, frozen room of ten thousand books, I said exactly what I thought but had not yet discovered.

"It must be nice," I told him, "coming from a tradition of theological scholarship, painstakingly hewed out over five hundred years since its inception in the remarkable thought of John Calvin, a friend and fellow Reformation leader with Martin Luther." Of course, this was why I had chosen that seminary. I wanted to be identified with that kind of theological history.

Then without thinking, I kept going. "Theology in my tradition stems from a bunch of mountain people rolling around in barns and shouting in tongues." I think I meant it to be funny, but the guy looked at me like I had just cursed his mother. He never uttered a word, just kept that scientific, touristy look on his face. I guess he thought I was serious. I guess I was.

I have now come to realize how much of my embarrassment was wrapped up in that conversation. It was not so much that I was ashamed of my church as I was ashamed that I was ashamed. Now, however, I am done being ashamed. I am plenty proud to be in the theological lineage of those mountain holy rollers, and the Presbyterians can have John Calvin's

Institutes of the Christian Religion and all the smart guys with beards, thank you very much.

Here is what I mean.

For quite a while now, writers of all sorts have been heralding the inauguration of a new, "postmodern" age. A lot of it is just hubbub to sell books, but this new way of thinking is valuable at its core, as it questions the presuppositions of the "modern" age, which began with the period known as the Enlightenment in the sixteenth century and produced such theologians as Martin Luther and John Calvin. The thinkers of the modern age broke away from previously held authorities in pursuit of consistent, rational thought. For some, this meant denouncing God and religion altogether. For Luther and Calvin, it meant denouncing the pope and all kinds of Roman Church practices that weren't explicitly found in Scripture. That was certainly well and good, but since that table had been swept clean and another one had to take its place, these reformers went about constructing lots of systematic, rational theology. They dissected the Bible into dozens of *-ologies*: soteriology, Christology, pneumatology . . . you name it, it had an *-ology*. Later systematizers even came up with catchy acronyms like T.U.L.I.P. to help people memorize these systems (Total depravity, Unconditional election, etc.). My teacher, the famous Old Testament scholar Walter Brueggemann, once said in class that John Calvin more or less wrote in his commentaries that certain segments of Scripture were just incorrect in order to get them to fit his theological matrix. At first glance, a theology like that brings plenty of stability, as the ongoing existence of Lutherans, Presbyterians, and other mainline Protestant groups attests. It weeds out a lot of the weird stuff in the Bible that makes us uncomfortable. Then again, these churches are also in steady decline. Looks like theological stability isn't so stable anymore.

By contrast, Pentecostal theology arose as the great middle finger to the tyranny of modernistic ideals. At the height of mainline liberal Protestantism in the early twentieth century, which went about "modernizing" and "demythologizing" the gospel stories by explaining away anything "irrational" (including miracles), Pentecostals were dancing, shouting, healing, and making themselves quite at home in the irrationality. Whereas modernism esteemed rationality, Pentecostals experienced the irrational power of God. Whereas modernism sought to control divinity in a thought matrix, Pentecostals didn't tame God. Whereas modernism built systems of church and ministry based on exclusion, Pentecostals were a band of anybodies and nobodies. Whereas modernism elevated experts, Pentecostals leveled the playing field.

In a description of the subversive Azusa Street Revival, which officially launched Pentecostal spirituality into existence at the beginning of the twentieth century, one of its early participants offered an apt description:

> Brother Seymour was recognized as the nominal leader in charge. But we had no pope or hierarchy. . . . The Lord himself was leading. . . . We did not honor men for their advantage, in means or education, but rather for their God-given "gifts" . . . The Lord was liable to burst through anyone. We prayed for this continually. Some one would finally get up anointed for the message. All seemed to recognize this and gave way. It might be a child, a woman, or a man.[1]

Who knew Pentecostals were so postmodern long before postmodernism?

"They admitted that they were aliens and strangers on earth," whoever wrote Hebrews said of the Old Testament faith heroes. What's worse, "They did not receive the things promised; they only saw them and welcomed them from a distance" (Heb 11:13). Undoubtedly, the heroes' great faith was rivaled only by their great embarrassment at such a predicament. Read their stories and you can still feel the sting of the jeers at their outrageous theology. Noah builds a boat without rain. Abraham claims a nation by raising a knife to the neck of his sole heir. Moses chooses disgrace over the royal court, then stammers and bumbles for the rest of his life. That kind of faith isn't born from memorizing a theological chart but from taking a ridiculous risk on a wild and often irreverent God. Pentecostal theology has been taking this risk from its beginning and it resonates.

Our word *embarrass*, in its contemporary sense, was first used in eighteenth-century France with regard to the wealthy. In books like *L'Embarras des richesses*, it referred to elites in a privileged dilemma: those who had more wealth than they knew what do with. All those years I was ashamed of my embarrassment, when I should have been embracing it. The mountain people in the barns came into a windfall, and the inheritance just keeps growing.

---

1. Cited in Harvey, *Freedom's Coming*, 132.

16

The End Times

What are all these fragments for, if not to be knit up finally?

—MARILYNN ROBINSON

It is hard to be a junior high student and a Pentecostal. Early adolescence is apocalyptic enough for atheists. Throw in what we believed about the "end times" of the world, which any minute might commence to tripwire the fiery judgment of God across the whole earth, and you've got yourself a recipe for many sleepless nights. The eschatology (belief in the end of time) that we passionately held was like sleeping with a live mortar round in your house, a spiritual minefield with terribly physical ramifications.

I remember a few of these early adolescent sleepless nights, and they were almost always connected to cursing. I said the F-word once when my sixth-grade girlfriend, Allison, broke up with me after a two-week sordid love affair during which we held hands once, in a screening of *The Little Mermaid*. I was sure that as a result hellfire and brimstone were just around the corner, because my church believed that a worldwide trumpet could sound at any moment to catch up the righteous to heaven, and if you'd sinned the second before then your ticket to glory just got a lot more expensive. That little slip might cost you seven years of tribulation and a severed head at the feet of the antichrist.

For the uninitiated, such a belief in the end of the world may sound strange, but at least it was specific. While Catholics believed in a "world without end," we Pentecostals believed in a definitive end, a big end. "The End. This story will self-destruct in five seconds." Ka-blam! The Big Bang all over again, but reversed.

⁂

The specifics of the end were stated in one of the points of my denomination's early Declaration of Faith: "We believe in the premillennial second coming of Jesus. First, to resurrect the righteous dead and to catch away the living saints to Him in the air. Second, to reign on the earth a thousand years." At first glance, this seems simple enough. Jesus will come back sometime in the future, right? Actually, we maintained that he will come back twice, and this is where things get hairy.

This concept of a dual messianic return is part of what is called dispensationalist theology, which was conceived by an Englishman named John Nelson Darby in the mid-nineteenth century. Although Darby's ideas were brand new to the scene, Pentecostals and most other evangelicals bought into them with great fervor. In Darby's schema of the end of the world, God would enact a seven-year "Tribulation Period," in which all hell would break loose on earth, led by a powerful global leader dubbed "The Antichrist" (in my childhood he was usually portrayed as the leader of the United Nations!). Wars would erupt. Famine would decimate the global population. Billions, literally, would die. This was the last chapter of God's plan for creation, according to Darby. After the world had been laid waste, Jesus would return to set up His kingdom on earth for a thousand years, before a final battle between good and evil at Armageddon. Then God would drop-kick creation into oblivion and everyone would be assigned to either heaven or hell. Darby saw all of this unfolding in the final book of the Bible, Revelation.

The bad news in all this was that God's plan was to annihilate the world. But the good news was that faithful Christians would be able to slip out the back door before the grand finale. To this end, we adhered to the idea of a "rapture" prior to the great tribulation—that Jesus would come down on a cloud and the saved would physically be raptured up to heaven. We'd been blowing all those shofars trying to get God to do His business down here, but soon Jesus would blow a trumpet and He'd carry us away in the nick of time. It could happen at any moment. The anticipation of the monumental event of the rapture was supposed to shape everything we did, so the earlier Pentecostals looked down on all kinds of frivolity. When my dad asked his parents if he could go skating, Grandpa's response was typical, but no less chilling. "I wouldn't want to be skating when Jesus comes back," he warned. My dad hedged his bets and went anyway. I was never so bold a gambler.

The rapture was the Christian's way off the Titanic—your last shot to get out of this world before God consumed everything and everyone with His wrath. The rapture was a stay of execution just before the switch was flipped. Things were all going to pot, but God loved us enough to get us the heck out of here first. This quick exit was not something you wanted to miss for a skating party.

No other medium reinforced this view of the end times with a greater potency than Christian films. Since these Christian groups never had any money for real actors or special effects, the movies always centered on the rapture of ordinary people to heaven. The plots were typical. A kid who had just said the F-word arrived home to find the blender on and a hot meal on the table—but no one else in the house, just several sets of clothes perfectly starched onto the furniture, remnants of those who were taken. I don't know any Pentecostal kid who didn't at some point arrive home to an empty house and almost lose his lunch thinking that the thing had happened. And it doesn't stop at childhood. The first time I heard the melodic siren of the tornado alarm in my Chicago suburb during graduate school, it crossed my mind that perhaps Jesus was blowing the rapture trumpet. I couldn't stop thinking about whether or not I had my house in order. This stuff really sticks with you.

Yet even when watching these movies I kept wondering why the raptured left their clothes behind on their way to heaven, and thinking about all those naked people at the same time was surely another sin in itself. The accumulation of such iniquities hit me late in my junior high years. I was visiting my grandparents in Tampa and the sunset pitched the sky all afire; it blazed in deep, unnatural tones behind clouds that lined up like staircases to that world beyond. My cousin and I were so taken aback by the sight that he asked me if I was ready for the coming of the Lord, since it looked like it might just be any second now. I sheepishly said yes, but in my heart I was terrified. The rapture was nothing to toy with, and here I had been spending my early adolescence cussing over girls and thinking about naked saints.

The clearest scriptural evidence we have for the rapture is in chapter 4 of 1 Thessalonians, the earliest New Testament document. There, the question is not really about the end of the world but what happens to the dead now that they're dead. The early Christians apparently never expected their own to die before the second coming of Christ, probably because initially Paul didn't either. Nevertheless, Paul tells them not to worry too much about it in view of where God is taking things.

> For this we say unto you by the word of the Lord, that we which are alive and remain unto the coming of the Lord shall not prevent them which are asleep. For the Lord himself shall descend from heaven with a shout, with the voice of the archangel, and with the trump of God: and the dead in Christ shall rise first: Then we which are alive and remain shall be caught up together with them in the clouds, to meet the Lord in the air: and so shall we ever be with the Lord. Wherefore comfort one another with these words. (1 Thess 4:15–18)

The Thessalonians were bent out of shape about their dead getting left out of the rapture, which was only for those who are "alive and remain." Paul says everyone will be at the party in the clouds for a meeting that won't end. He doesn't know when this will be any more than Jesus did ("About that day or hour no one knows . . ." [Mark 13:32]), but just the promise is enough to get by on. If the stressed out Thessalonian Christians keep reminding one another of this coming rapture, they'll get the comfort they need.

The peacefulness of Paul's depiction of the rapture has haunted me for some time. See, you get accustomed to dealing with God on the basis of His intention to snub you, and it's jarring when the Bible tells you you've been an idiot. The cadences of the very words in this passage strike me as wholly serene, with the rapture being a message of abiding comfort. Not motivation, not awe, not even anticipation, but comfort. Jesus will wrap his people in the clouds, like a baby tucked in for the night in the soft bassinette beside the parents' bed, and everything empty in us will be filled. If it's true, maybe those movies have been really misleading about God and his story for the world.

❧

I remember when my wife had our first child, a girl. We named her Sophia, which means "wisdom" in New Testament Greek. So far, raising a small child is kind of like winning the lottery day after day after day, with the joy compounded by the fact that no one ever told you just how wonderful the whole thing would be. If I had a quarter for every time some well-meaning parent told me that my life was "about to be turned upside down," I could have stocked Fort Knox by now. Of course it has been lots of work, but all the talk shows, seminars, and parenting books convince you that you're training for the heavyweight title. Then finally the announcer announces and the bell rings, but you throw your gloves to the ground because you realize it's not a fight at all. All the bravado was a sham, overpowered by the beauty, goodness, and wonder that is grace in a diaper.

Babies don't yet have a sense of time, beyond whatever might mark bedtime at night and waking in the morning. The tempo of these mark-ings forms something of the holiness around parenting, like tending a farm throughout its various seasons. The days may be filled with new and even chaotic activities, but these adventures are hedged between the two rou-tines that do not change in our house and thus have become sacred to us. No matter what happens each day, everyone knows how it will end and how it will begin again.

These endings are just around nightfall, after dinner has been eaten and plenty of time has been given to romping around on the carpet, read-ing stories, and staring at the moon. After finishing her milk, she gives me a kiss and Mom takes her up into her arms. Sophia locks her eyes on mine the second she is taken up, and Mom stops just before turning out of view into the hall. It is this brief hallowed pause, this secret moment where time seems to stand still, that I will take to my grave. Extending her arm toward me, Sophia and I stare and wave at each other until Mom makes the slow turn and the wall blocks our view. And all is well with the world.

"Comfort one another with these words," Paul says, because the One who you long for and who longs for you has been hidden for a time in that fuzzy in-between state before sleep, between day and night. And even though you have a sense that your eyes are still locked, you cannot see Him directly, the night will be longer than you would wish, and there will be sleep so deep that you will wonder if it is really sleep at all. You will imagine that the sleep is all that life is, that this great yearning will not be quenched outside of your dreams, but it's not true, no matter how dark the night.

On the heels of this great ending will come that distant beginning, when creation cannot hold back the news any longer, and that same air that Ephesians 2 tells us has been under the control of another ruler will be lifted from its fallenness as it receives back unto itself what has somehow kept it all together to begin with. And all will be well with the world.

I always heard, of course, that this grand reunion Paul describes in 1 Thessalonians is just a moment on the tour bus to heaven, but in fact he doesn't say a word about heaven in this passage. Read alongside the conventions of Roman history, Paul is actually using specific language about imperial visitations of his time. When the emperor (who was hailed as the "Son of God," by the way) scheduled an official visit to a particular city in the empire, strict codes of welcome were followed. These included first and foremost "meeting" the emperor outside of the city—the same word Paul uses—in order to receive him with great trumpets and fanfare, *and then to escort him into the gates.* By all indications Paul had this in mind.

New Testament Scholar John Dominic Crossan describes the consequences of this interpretation:

> Paul says nothing about an eschatological world or utopian earth here below, but simply that all believers "will be caught up in the clouds . . . to meet the Lord in the air; and so we will be with the Lord for ever." The [arrival] of the Lord was not about destruction of earth and relocation to heaven, but about a world in which violence and injustice are transformed into purity and holiness.[1]

If this is all so, then maybe it frees the rapture to really live up to its name— not some slick exit down the fire escape before all is lost, but the followers of Jesus truly *rapt*, engrossed and immersed in the consummation that is the very dawn of the new age. Really, it is a romantic term that somehow captures the exhale, the sighs of two people who have finally lost themselves in that embrace that they have been racing toward for too long.

Of course, we should not expect the world's response to Christ's second coming to be terribly unlike its response to the first. It shouldn't surprise us that Paul tells the other side of the story. Some will refuse to accept the new age. They will long for the "peace and safety" (1 Thess 5:3) of the old pecking order of competition, scarcity, and violence. They will not know how to

---

1. Crossan and Reed, *In Search of Paul*, 170.

function outside of this previous system. Like the confusion at the Tower of Babel in Genesis 11, for them the second coming upsets all they have built. Yet the fact that through Christ's second coming God will tear the monstrosity down is good news for the world, awfully and terribly good. Finally, as God pronounced in Genesis 1, creation will be truly good again, the joyful domain of creator and created, the boundless playground of father and child. At long last, the hungering morning will swallow the darkness.

Julian of Norwich, a medieval Christian mystic, said that God once spoke these words to her: "And all shall be well. And all shall be well. And all manner of things shall be well."

Just at dawn the cooing starts. Dabbling around with the things in her crib for a while, somehow Sophia doesn't even need to look at the door. I have cracked it ever so slightly and silently at times when she was looking away, yet she seems to have a sense for it beyond vision, and as she catches my eye in that tiny opening between the door and the wall, there is an exuberant sigh of relief, followed by the jumping joy of morning as I slowly open the door. Humming a melody while lifting the window shade with Sophia in my arms, a new day begins as it should begin, rapt in the warmth of the sun, rapt in one another, rapt in the radiance of the goodness that is the end of the long night and the start of what we can only guess about.

It is hardly strange that the Bible concludes its final sentence by weeping this wild hope, this hope that could be lost if it were elaborated any more, if it were spoken beyond a whisper, if it were codified into charts and graphs and novels. "Come, Lord Jesus." Even as we're lacing up our roller skates, come.

17

Community

The following are the rules they lay down: "Let no one come to us who has been educated, or who is wise or prudent (for we deem such qualifications unnecessary); but if there be any ignorant, or unintelligent, or uninstructed, or foolish persons, let them come into our fellowship with confidence." By which words, acknowledging that such individuals are worthy of their God, the Christians manifestly show that they desire and are able to win over only the silly, and the mean, and the stupid, the women and children.

—CELSUS, SECOND-CENTURY CRITIC OF CHRISTIANITY

Growing up Pentecostal gives you a wide array of eccentric acquaintances. The popular word now for Christian relationships is "community," which sounds so modern. Back then we called relationships within the church "fellowship," a stout term from the King James Bible. Fellowship was what you did when you hung out with other Pentecostals. It could be used as either a noun or a verb.

My first conception of Pentecostal fellowship originated with the friends from church whom I played with. One of these lived on our street, with a holiness mom who didn't wear pants or makeup, and perhaps as a result he was a relentless bully. Back then I certainly didn't get the connection between his religion and his anger. He was just the kid who condemned me for playing with He-Man, with all his sorcery that allowed his housecat to become a rideable tiger so that he could defeat Skeletor and the other evil guys. The bully played with GI Joe instead, who didn't use magic to slaughter the opposing forces of Cobra, which made it Pentecostal-Approved. We had an Irish tolerance for violence, what with our literal interpretation of the Old Testament, so the incongruity was lost to us.

The memories of our fellowship are legion. I turn the pages of the yearbook in my memory so easily. It is full of hobgoblins and angels, derelicts and dreamers, sinners and saints. There were shoeless boys with rat-tail haircuts, throwing butterfly knives around yards strewn with rusted car parts, whose friendship I enjoyed each year at church camp. There were the guitar-strummers, the musically and spiritually inclined, who skipped lunch at our Christian school to hold a tongues-infused prayer meeting for all the unpopular losers. There were the fatherless minority kids—blacks, Native Americans, Hispanics—for whom Pentecostal experience seemed so visceral and immediate. There was the old man on the front row, Earl, who would spin around like a one-man helicopter if the choir hit the right note, like he might ascend to heaven before us all. There was the miracles crowd, aficionados of the supernatural, to whom you best not admit any physical ailment, lest they lay hands on you in broad daylight. There were the charismatics who might interrupt any part of the worship service with a direct message from "thus saith the Lord." There were the new converts, rich and poor, young and old, who left their former lives at our altar to join this beautiful, disastrous family.

I can call them up at a moment's notice and they begin filing into the room: The people I have met while on these adventures in Pentecostal spirituality, the brothers and sisters who comprise my fellowship, my identity. "They come to the door of memory unannounced, stray dogs that amble in, sniff around a bit and simply never leave," Susan B. Anthony said, describing the truly important milestones of the past. "Our lives are measured by these."

Not all memories that the dogs drag in are pleasant. There was a Sunday school teacher who refused to have black children in the class (my best friend in elementary school was black). There was my friend from a prominent Pentecostal family who was jailed for grave crimes. There was another friend who told me once how deeply he hated his strict father, a well-known Pentecostal minister. I can still hear the cold passion in his voice.

All this and these are Pentecostalism. The fellowship cannot be edited to redefine the movement. I could serve up a list of Pentecostal doctrinal statements, but we arose as a reaction against the very notion of creeds. I could describe the sociology behind the rise of our growth, but this would be akin to describing the neurological chemical combustions behind the emergence of a love affair. What the dogs bring in is Pentecostalism as human story, because this is all it is and ever was. Pentecostalism is the extremity of raw humanity served up with a spiritual fervor—sort of like the Republican National Convention being held in the Superdome in the aftermath of Hurricane Katrina. Pentecostalism is helplessly human, painfully real.

In our day, homogeneity is one of the unstated requirements for the "successful" church. Visit a big church in the suburbs and this will be apparent. People will look the same, dress the same, and vote the same. Is this true Christian fellowship? If a Pentecostal church is homogenous, it probably isn't very Pentecostal. But make no mistake, we couldn't care less about the government's diversity campaigns. We are diverse because that's how our fellowship shakes out. We didn't engineer anything that way. Diversity happened as we simply tried to live according to the vision of the New Testament.

In his groundbreaking study of the archaeology of the early urban centers of the Christian movement, Peter Oakes reconstructs the setting of the first church of Rome. This is before cathedrals and church buildings, before pastors and ordained leaders, before all of the trappings and terms of "Christianity." Believers and seekers alike met in homes, perhaps thirty or forty at a time. We don't know anywhere near as much as we'd like to about what they did. We know that they gathered around the Eucharist and they sang hymns. Perhaps there were some readings from the Old Testament. It would be so precious to know these things, to have a grainy recording, a description of how it all worked.

What we can know, according to Oakes, is the composition of these early congregations, and he brings the setting vividly to life. They meet in the home/workshop of the craftworker, Holconius, who serves as the group's patron, thirty members cramming into three hundred square feet. The space is "spartan; dark if the doors were closed, open to the street if they were open; in a very noisy environment; heavily encumbered with materials, tools and work in progress; lacking in cooking facilities and latrine."[1] It smells bad in the room. There are a few other householders present, but the great majority of the group consists of slaves, freedmen, migrant workers, and the homeless. We meet some of these spiritual ancestors of ours. There is Primus, the Gentile slave. There is Sabina, a freed slave, scrapping for survival in the wake of being released by the master who had formerly provided for at least her basic physical needs. There is Iris, the barmaid, rented out for sex. And there is Holconius, the householder, a cabinetmaker thrust into a sense of responsibility for whatever this fellowship was, and whatever it was to become.

These are all the "many brothers and sisters" of Jesus Christ, the firstborn, according to one of the earliest Christian letters written to them (Rom 8:29). Oakes points out the thick irony of such a designation:

> If someone such as Holconius had been asked to picture a group of people answering to the description that Paul gives in Romans, the picture would not look like that group in the workshop, including his own slaves and children, the pair of stoneworkers who were scrabbling for subsistence, and the rather dubious serving girl from the bar down the street. Surely the Spirit-filled children of God ought to be a carefully selected group living a contemplative life in a temple on an island somewhere? Paul said that the Christians were indeed carefully chosen—but they turned out to be this lot![2]

When this context of the early Christian fellowships becomes real to us, the community rule of the New Testament seems far less trite. "We are all God's sons and daughters" (Rom 8:16). "You are all one in Christ Jesus" (Gal 3:28). "He has abolished the dividing wall of hostility" (Eph 2:14). Nothing sounded sweet or trite against the backdrop of Holconius's workshop. Those statements of fellowship sounded like a bomb exploding.

What Oakes is describing is not just the early gatherings of house churches. He is describing the core of Pentecostal Christianity today. The on-the-ground reality of the Pentecostal movement today is the same as it was for the early house churches: small fellowships of Christians crammed in dark rooms, discovering what it means to unremember everything that the wider culture says has value, and learning to dismantle every dividing wall between each of us.

1. Oakes, *Reading Romans in Pompeii*, 94–95.
2. Ibid., 165.

This is Pentecostalism, and Pentecostalism is no more definable than this: a story and a people. I have made some futile attempts in these pages, though less to define than to capture the moving targets of Pentecostal definition. The only definition of Pentecostalism that does not come up woefully short is the human story and God's story and the fellowship that is formed from such stories. We are story people.

"But God chose the foolish things of the world to shame the wise," Paul wrote in 1 Corinthians 1. "God chose the weak things of the world to shame the strong. He chose the lowly things of this world and the despised things—and the things that are not—to nullify the things that are, so that no one may boast before him." That upheaval was what was going on in Snellville, and it is still going on in similar places around the world today. I hope this book has taken you, if but for a moment, to one of those places. I hope that you have stood wide-eyed upon the pews. I hope that you have found yourself tarrying.

"Even on my slaves, both men and women, I will pour out my Spirit in those days" (Joel 2:29).

Bibliography

Adelaja, Sunday. *Church Shift*. Lake Mary, FL: Charisma House, 2008.

Baldwin, James. *The Cross of Redemption: Uncollected Writings*. Edited by Randall Kenan. New York: Pantheon, 2010.

Barrett, David. "Statistics, Global." In *Dictionary of Pentecostal and Charismatic Movements*, edited by S. M. Burgess and G. B. McGee, 810–30. Grand Rapids: Zondervan, 1988.

Bartchy, S. Scott. "Who Should Be Called Father? Paul of Tarsus between the Jesus Tradition and *Patria Potestas*." *Biblical Theology Bulletin* 33 (2003) 135–47.

Berry, Wendell. *What Are People For? Essays*. Berkeley: Counterpoint, 2010.

Black, Daniel L., ed. *Minutes of the 70th International General Assembly of the Church of God*. Cleveland, TN: Church of God Publishing House, 2004.

Borg, Marcus J. *Jesus, a New Vision: Spirit, Culture, and the Life of Discipleship*. New York: HarperCollins, 1987.

———. *Speaking Christian: Why Christian Words Have Lost Their Meaning and Power—and How They Can Be Restored*. New York: HarperOne, 2011.

Bradshaw, David. "Augustine the Metaphysician." In *Orthodox Readings of Augustine*, edited by George E. Demacopoulos and Aristotle Papanikolaou, 227–51. Crestwood, NY: St. Vladimir's Seminary Press, 2008.

Bragg, Rick. *Ava's Man*. New York: Knopf, 2001.

Brueggemann, Walter. *Living Toward a Vision*. New York: United Church Press, 1987.

———. *Mandate to Difference: An Invitation to the Contemporary Church*. Louisville: Westminster John Knox, 2007.

———. *Sabbath as Resistance: Saying No to the Culture of Now*. Louisville: Westminster John Knox, 2014.

Buber, Martin. *I and Thou*. New York: Touchstone, 1970.

Buechner, Frederick. *The Alphabet of Grace*. San Francisco: Harper & Row, 1970.

Chesterton, G. K. *Heretics*. New York: Barnes and Noble, 2007.

———. *Orthodoxy*. New York: Barnes & Noble, 2007.

Conzelmann, Hans. *The Theology of St. Luke*. Translated by Geoffrey Buswell. Philadelphia: Fortress, 1982.

Cox, Harvey. *Fire from Heaven: The Rise of Pentecostal Spirituality and the Reshaping of Religion in the Twenty-First Century*. New York: Addison-Wesley, 1995.

Crossan, John Dominic, and Jonathan L. Reed. *In Search of Paul: How Jesus's Apostle Opposed Rome's Empire with God's Kingdom*. New York: HarperCollins, 2004.

Dawkins, Richard. *The God Delusion*. New York: Mariner, 2006.

Devoe, Richard F. *Christianity and the Roman Games: The Paganization of Christians by Gladiators, Charioteers, Actors and Actresses from the First through the Fifth Centuries A.D.* Bloomington, IN: Xlibris, 2003.

Dillard, Annie. *For the Time Being*. New York: Vintage, 1999.

———. *Teaching a Stone to Talk*. New York: HarperCollins, 1982.

Dorsett, Lyle W. *A Passion for Souls: The Life of D. L. Moody*. Chicago: Moody, 1997.

Ege, Richard A. *Finding My Way to Salvation: A Traditional Old Catholic Priest's View of the Past Fifty Years*. Victoria, BC: Friesen, 2013.

Eliot, T. S. *Four Quartets*. New York: Harcourt, Brace, 1943.

Emerson, Ralph Waldo. *The Essays of Ralph Waldo Emerson*. Cambridge: Harvard University Press, 1987.

Finney, Charles G. *How to Experience Revival*. New Kensington, PA: Whitaker House, 1984.

Foster, Richard. *Celebration of Discipline: The Path to Spiritual Growth*. New York: HarperCollins, 1988.

Friesen, Aaron T. *Norming the Abnormal: The Development and Function of the Doctrine of Initial Evidence in Classical Pentecostalism*. Eugene, OR: Pickwick, 2013.

Goheen, Michael W. *Introducing Christian Mission Today: Scripture, History and Issues*. Downers Grove, IL: InterVarsity, 2014.

Gurin, Patricia. "My Remembrance: The March on Washington." http://spectrumcenter. umich.edu/article/50th-anniversary-civil-rights-movement-reflection.

Hanson, Collin. "Young, Restless, and Reformed: Calvinism Making a Comeback and Shaking Up the Church." *Christianity Today*, September 2006, 32–38.

Harvey, Paul. *Freedom's Coming: Religious Culture and the Shaping of the South from the Civil War through the Civil Rights Era*. Chapel Hill: University of North Carolina Press, 2005.

Hauerwas, Stanley, and William H. Willimon. *Resident Aliens*. Nashville: Abingdon, 1989.

Herron, Fred. *No Abiding Place: Thomas Merton and the Search for God*. Lanham, MD: University Press of America, 2005.

Hunsberger, George R. "The Newbigin Gauntlet: Developing a Domestic Missiology for North America." In *The Church between Gospel and Culture: The Emerging Mission in North America*, edited by George R. Hunsberger, 3–25. Grand Rapids: Eerdmans, 1996.

Johns, Cheryl. "Preaching Pentecost to the Nones." *Journal for Preachers* 36 (2013) 3–10.

Jones, Peter Rhea. *Studying the Parables of Jesus*. Macon, GA: Smyth and Helwys, 1999.

Judge, Edwin. "St. Paul and Classical Culture." *Jahrbuch für Antike und Christentum* 15 (1980) 19–36.

Kanungo, Rabindra N., and Manuel Mendonca. *Ethical Dimensions of Leadership*. Thousand Oaks, CA: Sage, 1996.

Keener, Craig S. *Miracles: The Credibility of the New Testament Accounts*. 2 vols. Grand Rapids: Baker Academic, 2011.

Kennedy, D. James. *Evangelism Explosion*. 4th ed. Carol Stream, IL: Tyndale House, 1996.

Land, Steven J. *Pentecostal Spirituality: A Passion for the Kingdom*. Sheffield: Sheffield Academic, 1993.

Laurent, Olivier. "Filling the Pantheon with Selfies." June 12, 2014. http://time. com/2863216/filling-the-pantheon-with-selfies/.

Lewis, C. S. *The Complete C.S. Lewis Signature Classics*. New York: HarperOne, 2002.

Long, Eugene Thomas. *Twentieth-Century Western Philosophy of Religion, 1900–2000*. Boston: Kluwer Academic, 2003.

McClung, Grant. "Historical Perspectives: Introduction." In *Azusa Street and Beyond*, edited by Grant McClung, 1–22. Gainesville, FL: Bridge-Logos, 2006.

McCoy, Marjorie Casebier. *Frederick Buechner: Novelist and Theologian of the Lost and Found*. San Francisco: Harper & Row, 1988.

McKnight, Scot. "Who Are the NeoReformed? 2." http://www.beliefnet.com/columnists/jesuscreed/2009/02/who-are-the-neoreformed-2.html#.

Menzie, Nicola. "Pastor Wilfredo De Jesus Credits Church Growth to Serving the Marginalized." June 18, 2013. http://www.christianpost.com/news/pastor-wilfredo-de-jesus-credits-church-growth-to-serving-the-marginalized-98244/.

Merton, Thomas. *Thoughts in Solitude*. New York: Farrar, Straus and Giroux, 1999.

Miller, Lisa. "BeliefWatch: Spirit Filled." November 5, 2006. http://www.newsweek.com/beliefwatch-spirit-filled-107031.

Nouwen, Henri J. M. *Life of the Beloved: Spiritual Living in a Secular World*. New York: Crossroad, 1992.

Oakes, Peter. *Reading Romans in Pompeii: Paul's Letter at Ground Level*. Minneapolis: Fortress, 2013.

O'Connor, Flannery. *A Prayer Journal*. New York: Farrar, Straus and Giroux, 2013.

Philips. J. B. *Your God Is Too Small*. New York: Touchstone, 2004.

Philo, of Alexandria. *Selected Writings*. Edited by Hans Lewy. Mineoloa, NY: Dover, 2004.

Pinnock, Clark. *Flame of Love: A Theology of the Holy Spirit*. Downers Grove, IL: IVP Academic, 1996.

Poloma, Margaret. *Main Street Mystics: The Toronto Blessing and Reviving Pentecostalism*. Walnut Creek, CA: AltaMira, 2003.

Potok, Chaim. *The Promise*. New York: Anchor, 2005.

Powell, Mark Allan. *Loving Jesus*. Minneapolis: Fortress, 2004.

Rhoads, David. *The Challenge of Diversity: The Witness of Paul and the Gospels*. Minneapolis: Fortress, 1996.

Rice, Joshua. *Paul and Patronage: The Dynamics of Power in 1 Corinthians*. Eugene, OR: Pickwick, 2013.

Rilke, Rainer Maria. *Letters to a Young Poet*. Translated by M. D. Herter Norton. New York: Norton, 1934.

Selig, Jennifer Leigh. *Thinking Outside the Church: 110 Ways to Connect with Your Spiritual Nature*. Kansas City: Andrews McMeel, 2004.

Smith, Zadie. *NW: A Novel*. New York: Penguin, 2013.

Sweet, Leonard I. *The Greatest Story Never Told: Revive Us Again*. Nashville: Abingdon, 2012.

Synan, Vinson. *The Holiness-Pentecostal Tradition: Charismatic Movements in the Twentieth Century*. Grand Rapids: Eerdmans, 1971.

Tillich, Paul. *The New Being*. Lincoln: University of Nebraska Press, 2005.

———. *The Shaking of the Foundations*. New York: Scribner's, 1948.

Tucker, J. Brian. *You Belong to Christ: Paul and the Formation of Social Identity in 1 Corinthians 1–4*. Eugene, OR: Pickwick, 2010.

Twain, Mark. *Adventures of Huckleberry Finn*. Mineoloa, NY: Dover, 1994.

———. *Mark Twain's Own Autobiography: The Chapters from the North American Review*. Madison: University of Wisconsin Press, 1990.

Bibliography

Wesley, John. *The Essential Works of John Wesley.* Edited by Alice Russie. Uhrichsville, OH: Barbour, 2011.

———. *The Journal of the Reverend John Wesley, A.M.* Vol. 1. New York: Carlton and Philips, 1855.

White, John. *When the Spirit Comes with Power: Signs and Wonders among God's People.* Downers Grove, IL: InterVarsity, 1988.

Wright, N.T. "Apocalyptic and the Beauty of God." A sermon at Harvard Memorial Church, October 22, 2006. http://ntwrightpage.com/sermons/Harvard_Beauty.htm.

Made in the USA
Lexington, KY
18 November 2015